RAILWAYS IN EAST YORKSHIRE
VOLUME TWO

Martin Bairstow

Ex North Eastern Railway Class G6 0-4-4T, then nearly 60 years old, arriving at Willerby & Kirk Ella with a local from Hull to South Howden in March 1955. *(J.C.W. Halliday)*

Published by Martin Bairstow, Fountain Chambers, Halifax, West Yorkshire
Printed by Amadeus Press Ltd, Huddersfield, West Yorkshire

Introduction

In the introduction to *Railways in East Yorkshire,* written just five years ago, I held out the hope that one day there might be a second volume. Here it is and I am pleased to welcome guest contributions from David R. Smith, John Bateman, Bill Smith, Richard Pulleyn and Tony Ross to which I have added some chapters of my own.

As before, the geographical limits of East Yorkshire have been interpreted rather liberally so as to embrace a wide area beginning at Leeds and including the coast from Scarborough to Withernsea. A detailed map, drawn by John Holroyd, appears on the centre pages of *Railways in East Yorkshire.* The map below gives a general outline.

Thanks are due to all contributors. The articles and photographs are credited individually. The tickets and excursion handbills are from the collections of Geoffrey Lewthwaite and David Beeken respectively. John Holroyd has again helped with artwork, in particular the removal of scratches and other imperfections on the photographs. Stuart Carmichael lent me his darkroom to print some of the negatives which were too large for my equipment. Richard Pulleyn provided the signal diagrams. Dennis Coward spared me a morning to recall his days at Stoneferry. The manuscript was typed by Glynis Boocock.

Thanks also to my wife Philippa for accompanying me on a number of trips to the area in search of material.

Railways in East Yorkshire sold out at the end of 1994. If there is evidence of demand, consideration will be given to a new edition which will appear as *Railways in East Yorkshire Volume One.* It may be possible to enlarge it slightly. If anybody has any material which they feel must be included then please submit it quickly. In particular has anybody a photograph of Stoneferry Box or Sigglesthorne Station? Intermediate photographs on the Hornsea and Withernsea lines have proved very elusive.

I am also working on *Railways Around Whitby Volume Two* and would be very pleased to consider any material which readers may be able to offer whether in the form of memories or photographs.

Martin Bairstow

Halifax, West Yorkshire
August 1995

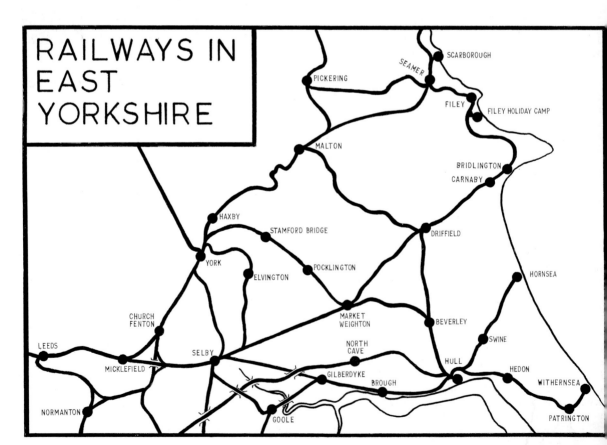

Trans-Pennine (or Coast to Coast)

The 12.50 Hull to Leeds passing Ferriby on 26 July 1979. The 'Trans Pennine' units ended their days in 4 coach formation merged with Swindon Cross Country sets.
(G. W. Morrison)

Railways in East Yorkshire (volume one 1990 edition), concluded with the words '. . . BR Provincial Sector is not devoid of new ideas. If the class 158 air conditioned 'sprinters' prove to have been worth waiting for then there should be more interesting times ahead'.

For Provincial Sector read Regional Railways North East though who knows what it will be called if/when it is franchised. Setting that speculation aside, whoever does continue the Class 158 operated 'Trans Pennine' service will be taking over an operation which has seen radical change in recent years.

We are not, in this book, concerned with the trebling of train service frequency over the central part of the 'Trans Pennine' route between Leeds and Manchester but with the development and extension of regular interval trains eastwards from Leeds.

The brand name 'Trans Pennine' seems to have entered the vocabulary to describe the diesel service introduced on 2 January 1961 between Hull, Leeds, Manchester and Liverpool. Prior to that date, there had only been three through trains each weekday from Hull to Liverpool and two the other way. Departures from Hull were at 9.00, 14.02, and 16.00 returning from Liverpool Lime Street at 11.00

and 15.50. Journey time varied between $3^{1}/_{2}$ and 4 hours for the $126^{1}/_{4}$ miles.

Against this background, the 1961 diesel service was something of an innovation. The 'Planning and Execution' was described in *Trains Illustrated* for April 1961. Apparently in those days, 'the instigator of cross country improvements' which straddled a regional boundary 'had to be patient through negotiation that may be as protracted as the nuclear test-ban discussions at Geneva'.

The new 'Trans Pennine' service was an initiative of the North Eastern Region whose territory extended as far as the east end of Standedge Tunnel. It was based on a departure at 45 minutes past each hour from Leeds to Liverpool.

Six trains started from Hull at 9.13, 10.43, 12.10, 13.41, 15.43 and 17.53. Having negotiated so patiently with his London Midland Region colleague to establish a regular interval pattern to Manchester and Liverpool, the North Eastern timetable planner had only mixed success in extending the principle through his own territory to Hull.

The 9.13 departure was so timed to connect with trains from Bridlington, Hornsea and Withernsea and this went forward from Leeds to Liverpool at 10.15 as an extra to the hourly service. The 12.10 stopped at most stations to Leeds whence it formed

A Hull to Liverpool 'Trans Pennine' arriving at Selby on 7 August 1976. *(Tom Heavyside)*

45132 negotiates the curves through Kirkham Abbey with a train from Scarborough on 12 June 1976.
(Tom Heavyside)

the 13.45 to Liverpool. The 17.53 was even worse running slow to Leeds then waiting 18 minutes before continuing at 19.45.

That only left three departures from Hull which fitted into the regular interval sequence, stopping at Brough and Selby, reaching Leeds in one hour and Liverpool in three.

The rolling stock was no less revolutionary. $8^{1/2}$ six car 'Trans Pennine' dmus were delivered to Neville Hill for the Hull – Liverpool service. Each set comprised four powered and two trailer coaches with a total of eight 230hp engines providing seating for 300 passengers. The two end carriages were 'open' with all seats facing the driving compartment giving an excellent forward view from the first class saloon. Next to these were two powered second class compartment coaches with brake van and luggage space. In the middle of the train were the two trailers. One was an open second, the other was part buffet but also had three first-class compartments plus a first-class lavatory which was twice as large as the six normal loos found elsewhere on the train.

Six sets were rostered to work the weekday service which left two and a half in reserve. All were based at Neville Hill, Leeds, but one was stabled overnight at Hull and another at Liverpool. There was a limited service on Sundays but not from Hull.

Publicity for the 'Inter-City' Diesel Service' offered 'A new standard of cross country travel'. It went on to extoll the 'unique griddle car providing hot snacks and light meals, freshly cooked on the griddle' . . . 'It's new, it's quicker, it's more comfortable'.

Four of the hourly Leeds to Liverpool trains were diesel loco hauled and these came through from Newcastle. Two went via Harrogate and the other two via York. Initially these did not stop at York though by 1964 they were doing so. After closure of the Northallerton to Harrogate line in 1967, they all had to go via York.

In an editorial on 'Trans Pennine' services, *Modern Railways* for November 1968 dismissed 'such places as York' as 'towns with no growth potential in themselves which impede attack on longer distance markets'. That ludicrous comment was probably quite close to contemporary BR thinking in which case things really have changed since those depressing post-Beeching years.

The 1961 'Trans Pennine' service functioned with little change for 18 years. By 1979, the diesel sets had lost much of their gloss as well as their 'griddle cars'. The reduced five coach formations, four of them theoretically powered, providing greater insurance against engine failures.

The introduction of High Speed Trains on the East Coast Main Line allowed the transfer in May 1979 of Type 4 locos and early Mark 2 (non air conditioned) coaches to the 'Trans Pennine' service. This was recast as an hourly interval from Liverpool to York with some workings extended to Newcastle. Hull was left with an hourly connecting service

provided by four car hybrid sets created out of 'Trans Pennine' and 'Swindon Cross County' units. It was in this guise that the 'Trans Pennines' struggled on until the mid 1980s.

A new development came in January 1982 when most of the trains not going to Newcastle were extended through from York to Scarborough. Previously the Spa Town had relied on connections by local dmu from Leeds or York.

The next significant change came in May 1987 with the introduction of the first 'sprinter' sets on an enhanced frequency giving a train every half hour between Leeds and Manchester. One train per hour was through from Hull, the other from York having originated on alternate hours from Newcastle or Scarborough.

The two hourly Newcastle – Liverpool was loco hauled, the remaining 3/4 of the service was in the hands of class 150/2 'Sprinters'. These were inadequate of class with high density but low seats, very uncomfortable for people with long legs. They were however, only a stop gap until the superior Class 156 'Supersprinters' began to appear from 1988.

This lasted only three years. From May 1990, the Leeds – Manchester frequency was increased again to three trains per hour; one from Hull, one from Scarborough and the other from Newcastle on alternate hours, otherwise just from York. This leap forward should have coincided with the introduction of air conditioned 'Sprinters' of Class 158 but these were delayed for almost a year leaving odd gaps in the service pattern which was otherwise maintained by units of Class 156 with loco haulage from Newcastle.

Gradually the 158s did turn up and it was not long before the next expansion in service. May 1993 saw the alternate hour York – Liverpool starting at Middlesbrough and the hourly Scarborough – Manchester going through to the new station at Manchester Airport.

This pattern lasted for only 12 months. From May 1994 the Middlesbrough service was increased to hourly running through to Manchester Airport. The Liverpool train then started alternately from Newcastle and from Scarborough. The resultant gap on the Scarborough line was filled by upgrading the hourly Leeds – Blackpool train from a Class 155 to a 158 and incorporating it into the 'Trans Pennine' network starting every two hours from Scarborough and on the other hour from York, in both cases stopping at Garforth. The hourly Hull to Manchester Piccadilly train continues to run hourly with stops at Brough and Selby.

A by product of the Airport link has been the introduction of night trains. It was realised that a 'normal' first departure from York at (say) 6am would get people to the Airport after many of the flights had gone. In the 1994/5 timetable there are trains from York to Manchester Airport at 2.38, 3.48, 5.00, 6.18 then 7.18 which is the first one through from Middlesbrough then hourly until 21.21 and a late one at 23.08. In the reverse direction, there are

Scarborough joined the 'Trans Pennine' network in 1982. 45144 arrives with the 9.03a.m. from Liverpool Lime Street on 25 April 1987.
(Tom Heavyside)

45040 arrives at York with a Liverpool to Scarborough train on 28 June 1986. 47488 waits to take over from the Class 45.
(Tom Heavyside)

departures from Manchester Airport for York at 23.28, 2.13, 5.13 then more or less hourly through the day. The night trains also allow travel between York, Leeds, Huddersfield and Manchester Piccadilly and have attracted some non-airport traffic.

With a train every two hours from Scarborough to Liverpool, and one on the alternate hour to Blackpool, 'Trans Pennine' has now become a true Coast to Coast operation. The significant factor is not the number of people travelling right through but the journey opportunities created by a regular interval service linking important centres of population.

Journeys such as York to Burnley, Accrington or Blackburn can be made hourly each weekday, two hourly on Sundays. Prior to 1984, this was impossible at all by rail. Scarborough to Huddersfield or Manchester is now every two hours by through train, hourly if you don't mind the single change. Traditionally, there was no through service except on summer Sundays or excursions. A more routine journey would have involved changes at York and/or Leeds between services which were not necessarily planned with connections in mind.

All trains are scheduled to be operated by Class 158 air conditioned 'sprinters' capable of running at up to 90mph. Most formations are of only two or three coaches and may look rather modest compared to the long loco hauled trains of the past. They are, however, of much higher capacity with no first class or van space, and they do run more frequently. But who invented seat bottoms which become detached from their fixtures and which can have pieces of metal projecting from them? My wife recovered the cost of a new pair of tights together with an explanation from Regional Railways North East that there was a design fault with the seats.

Long gone are the days of the griddle car but most trains now convey a refreshment trolley for at least part of their journey.

The new order on 'Trans Pennine' 158746 leaving Hull on the 13.40 to Manchester Piccadilly, 16 May 1991.
(Tom Heavyside)

And the new destination. 15856 awaits departure from Manchester Airport with the 16.28 to Scarborough on 7 May 1994.   *(Martin Bairstow)*

Garforth joined the 'Trans Pennine' network in May 1994 when the hourly York (or Scarborough) to Blackpool service began to stop there. A York to Leeds local calls in May 1977. *(Martin Bairstow)*

B16 4-6-0 No. 61418 pulling into Church Fenton with the 3.10p.m. York-Leeds express on 27 February 1960. This was the only stop. *(M. Mitchell)*

B1 4-6-0 No. 61069 east of Malton with a Saturdays only Manchester Victoria to Scarborough on 4 August 1962. The Driffield branch is on the left. *(A. M. Ross)*

No 517

Great Yorkshire Show at Hull

Day Excursion
to York Scarborough & Hull
Thursday, 17th July

					Return Fares			
					To York	To Scarbro'	To Hull	
					3rd	3rd	1st	3rd
				a.m.				
Hawes	...	...	... dep.	6 10	6/6	8/6	15/-	9/-
Askrigg	...	...	,,	6 15	6/-	8/-	15/-	9/-
Aysgarth	...	...	,,	6 25	5/6	8/-	14/6	8/6
Redmire	...	...	,,	6 30	5/6	8/-	14/6	8/6
Wensley	...	...	,,	6 35	5/-	7/6	14/6	8/6
Leyburn	...	...	,,	6 45	5/-	7/6	13/6	8/-
Spennithorne	...	...	,,	6 50	5/-	7/6	13/6	8/-
Constable Burton	...	...	,,	6 55	4/6	7/6	13/6	8/-
Finghall Lane	...	...	,,	7 0	4/6	7/6	13/6	8/-
Jervaulx	...	...	,,	7 5	4/-	7/-	13/6	8/-
Crakehall	...	...	,,	7 10	4/-	7/-	13/6	8/-
Bedale	...	...	,,	7 15	4/-	7/-	12/6	7/6
Leeming Bar	...	...	,,	7 20	4/-	6/6	12/6	7/6
Scruton	...	...	,,	7 25	3/6	6/6	12/6	7/6
Ainderby	...	...	,,	7 30	3/6	6/6	12/6	7/6
Northallerton	...	...	,,	7 45	3/-	6/-	12/6	7/6
Otterington	...	...	,,	7 50	3/-	5/6	12/-	7/-
Thirsk	...	...	,,	8 0	2/6	5/6	11/-	6/6
York	...	...	,,	8 40	—	4/6	A	
							a.m.	
	Arrival times	...	...				10 16	

A—See separate bills.

Passengers for Hull change at York in each direction, on the outward journey going forward at 9-10 a.m.

RETURN ARRANGEMENTS.—The train will return the same day from Hull 6-25 p.m., Scarborough (Central Station) 6-25 p.m., York 7-30 p.m., arriving Northallerton 8-15 p.m., Leyburn 9-15 p.m. and Hawes 10-0 p.m.

TICKETS CAN BE OBTAINED IN ADVANCE

Tickets, bills and all particulars can be obtained at the stations or from Messrs. T. Cook & Son, Ltd., York (Tel. No. 2486).

For further information apply to the District Passenger Manager, York (Tel. No. 2264).

The East Yorkshire Motor Services will run a frequent service of buses between Paragon Station Yard and the Show Ground each day

FOR CONDITIONS OF ISSUE SEE OTHER SIDE

YORK, June, 1930.

London & North Eastern Railway

37214—Ben Johnson & Co., Ltd., Printers, York—2,500.

LONDON AND NORTH EASTERN RAILWAY

London and North Eastern Railway Temperance Union

On Wednesday, 8th August, 1923

EXCURSION TO

Scarborough & Bridlington

FARES	TO SCARBOROUGH, 2/-
	FROM NEWCASTLE AND GATESHEAD TO BRIDLINGTON, 3/-
	FROM OTHER STATIONS TO BRIDLINGTON, 2/-

NEWCASTLE TO SCARBOROUGH AND BRIDLINGTON.

NEWCASTLE	............dep	6 15 a.m.
GATESHEAD WEST	,,	6 18 ,,
DURHAM	,,	6 50 ,,
FERRYHILL	,,	7 12 ,,
DARLINGTON	,,	7 40 ,,

RETURNING FROM BRIDLINGTON AT 5-30 p.m. AND SCARBOROUGH AT 6-35 p.m.

Passengers from Sunderland travel to Newcastle by 5-10 a.m., returning from latter place at 11-5 p.m.

HARTLEPOOL TO SCARBOROUGH.

HARTLEPOOL	............dep	6 25 a.m.
WEST HARTLEPOOL	,,	6 33 ,,
STOCKTON	,,	6 58 ,,
EAGLESCLIFFE	,,	7 6 ,,

RETURNING FROM SCARBOROUGH AT 6-45 p.m.

Passengers from MIDDLESBROUGH travel to STOCKTON by 6-28 a.m. on outward journey and from EAGLESCLIFFE on return.

Passengers to and from BRIDLINGTON change at SCARBOROUGH in each direction.

CROOK TO SCARBOROUGH.

CROOK	............dep	6 5 a.m.
BISHOP AUCKLAND	,,	6 28 ,,
SHILDON	,,	6 40 ,,

RETURNING FROM SCARBOROUGH AT 6-55 p.m.

Passengers to and from BRIDLINGTON change at SCARBOROUGH in each direction.

Tickets will be issued by the Committee only as follows:—On or before August 6th.—Newcastle—Mr. G. Williamson; Gateshead—Mr. A. Brown and Mr. C. Metcalfe (Secretary); Sunderland—Mr. L. Jackson; West Hartlepool—Mr. R. Newbold; Thornaby—Mr. T. Joplin; Stockton—Mr. A. E. Hunton; Middlesbrough—Mr. J. Stockdale; Darlington—Mr. T. Hancock; Shildon—Mr. S. Gardiner; Crook—Mr J. Buckle; Ferryhill—Mr R. Wilton; Durham—Mr. A. W. Shield.

(1). Each Railway Member of the Association will be allowed tickets for himself, wife, and such of his children as reside with and are dependent upon him. Each unmarried Railway Member not less than 18 years of age will be allowed, in addition to his own ticket, to have one for a female friend accompanying him.

(2). Children under 12 years of age, half-fare.

(3). The following regulations will be strictly enforced. Each Member must apply personally for the tickets required for himself, as one member will not be allowed to purchase tickets for another member.

(4). By special arrangement a limited number of tickets at a special fare will be issued to members of the Association who are not Railway employees.

(5). Any passenger not covered by the conditions shewn above, found in possession of a ticket issued for this train, travelling or attempting to travel by the train, will be prosecuted under the provisions of the Company's Bye-Laws in the same manner as a person travelling without a ticket, and the person (if a Railway Employee) to whom the ticket was originally issued will be instantly dismissed from the service of the Company.

(6). Any person obtaining tickets who is afterwards prevented from using them, can have his or her money returned on application to the person from whom the tickets were bought.

NO LUGGAGE ALLOWED.

Class 31 D5824 has just passed Malton with a Saturdays only Scarborough to Sheffield Victoria express on 4 August 1962. Ivatt 2-6-2T No. 41265 is the Malton station pilot. *(A. M. Ross)*

Prestige power on the Scarborough line. The summer Saturdays only Scarborough to Glasgow passing Haxby Road level crossing on 28 June 1986. *(Stuart Baker)*

A speculation

Was Withernsea just a run-down seaside town offering no potential to the modern railway? Or would trains now be busy with commuters and shoppers especially from some of the intermediate stations?
(John Marshall)

The 1964 General Election campaign was conducted just as the 'Beeching Axe' was coming into full swing. Yet although the programme of closures affected nearly every corner of the United Kingdom, the issue scarcely penetrated the hustings.

In truth, the Labour Opposition did not have any alternative policy. They just spoke vaguely about a moratorium on 'major closures' pending a Royal Commission on transport as a whole. They did not, however, do anything to discourage a view which was held fairly widely amongst their supporters especially railway staff that a change of Government would offer salvation for some threatened lines.

The election was held on Thursday 15 October and by the evening of Friday 16th, Harold Wilson had kissed hands with the Queen.

At once he received a telegram from the Clerk to Hornsea Urban District Council: "Hornsea and Withernsea branch lines close tomorrow night. Request you intervene to halt closure". – He didn't!

Writing in 1990 in the *North Eastern Express*, Pat Rington and S. Wine' speculate what might have happened if the decision had gone the other way, based on experience with developments elsewhere on BR.

If the two branches had earned a temporary reprieve in 1964, then they might have survived long enough to become part of Barbara Castle's basic railway in 1968 and to gain the protection of the PSO grant from 1974 onwards. It is probable that the frequency of service would have gone down at first but would have risen, possibly to an hourly interval on each branch with the advent of 'pacer' units in the late 1980s.

Goods traffic would still have disappeared and surplus railway land would have been sold off as would the station houses possibly generating some additional commuter traffic. Eventually the two branch termini would have been redeveloped with railway business transferred to previously abandoned excursion platforms outside the main structures. Station staff, if any, would be restricted to one person at each terminus on a morning shift only.

Most of the double track would have been reduced to single with all or nearly all signal boxes eliminated depending on what method was adopted to control the single lines. Level crossings would have been automated, possibly with financial assistance from the local authority as has happened on the Bridlington line. The same source of funding

Withernsea terminus on 19 September 1964. Had it remained open, one could imagine the main part of the station being redeveloped leaving railway business to be done at the platform nearer the middle of this photograph. *(John Marshall)*

A Cravens unit under the canopy at Hornsea Town. Again it is possible that, had the line survived, the station building would have been sold off and trains would have had to use the excursion platform upon which the photographer is standing. *(John Marshall)*

The island platform at Wilmington was opened on 9 June 1912 replacing both the 1864 Wilmington Station on the Hornsea branch and Sculcoates Station at the other side of the swing bridge. A Cravens dmu restarts for Hull.
(John Bateman Collection)

J5 No. 67280 descending the 1924 Walton Street curve by which H&B line passenger trains were diverted to Hull Paragon. The train is the 7.53a.m. from South Howden on 7 April 1955. *(John Oxley)*

might have helped with modest tidying up of the intermediate stations with improved lighting and simple shelters to replace redundant waiting rooms – usually on the platform opposite to the main building which would have been sold off.

A possible reason why the Ministry of Transport ignored the 1964 TUCC findings that closure would cause hardship was their determination to eliminate level crossings in the Hull area – not because it cost too much to operate them but in order to ease the flow of road traffic into the city centre.

'Pat Rington and S. Wine' suggest that by 1969 a reprieved passenger service would, like the remaining goods traffic, have been diverted on to the higher level Hull & Barnsley route allowing the level crossing ridden NE line to be abandoned. They point out that a spur from the H&B to the Hornsea branch was in fact built in 1968 though used only until 1971 and that traffic to King George Dock still crosses from the H&B to a short stretch of the Withernsea branch at Southcoates Junction. The question is how to get on to the H&B at the Hull Paragon end. Our correspondents suggest a curve climbing north east from the Bridlington line at Walton Junction onto the H&B which passes over. This would have involved crossing a cemetery and demolishing a few houses – a small price to pay for speeding up road traffic, at least by the standards of that pre-environmentally conscious period.

Stations could have been provided on the H&B route to replace those bypassed on the North Eastern. The increased journey time is estimated at only three minutes which would have been regained when 'pacers' were introduced 20 years later.

In conclusion, 'Pat Rington and S. Wine' suggest that retention of the two branches would have made only marginal difference to the towns of Hornsea and Withernsea. That may be so but, surely, the cost of retaining them would have been equally marginal in the overall context of transport expenditure. The operating costs, which formed the basis of the case for closure, were most certainly capable of reduction.

More than just idle speculation?

During the mid 1970s, the BR Area Manager at Hull was Chris Green, the gentleman who subsequently brought his own style of management successively to Scotrail, Network South East and Inter City. In 1995 he resigned from a second term at the head of Scotrail supposedly in protest at the privatisation shambles.

Whilst at Hull, he had members of his staff produce a scheme for reopening the Hornsea line as far as Sutton on Hull, which is close to the large Bransholme Estate, and the Withernsea line as far as Hedon. Trains would have run from Hull Paragon via the Hull & Barnsley route to which access was to be gained via Walton Street with reversal at Springbank North. A direct curve from Walton Street to the east was not contemplated.

According to *Modern Railways* (May 1976) 'the project was closely examined by the County Council as part of its long term transport plans but it is unlikely to be developed in the immediate future'. Perhaps the idea was ahead of its time as the handful of local authority sponsored line reopenings which have taken place did not begin until Edinburgh to Bathgate in 1986.

I venture to suggest that some day there will, at the very least, be consideration given to a light railway system in Hull. In which case somebody may notice the long stretches of disused former railway lines reaching out from the edge of the city towards the dormitory towns of Hornsea and Withernsea.

The route from Paragon station would not involve a semi-circular sweep around the city either by the NE nor by the H&B, but would set off in a direct line through a traffic calmed shopping and commercial centre.

The level crossings would have had to be modernised but this had been proposed as part of the CTC scheme which was to have been pioneered on the York to Beverley line then extended. Ryehill & Burstwick looking back towards Hull.
(John Birkbeck

Standard Class 3 2-6-0 No. 77010 passing Swine with an 'express' for Hull on the evening of Sunday 31 July 1955. *(John Oxley)*

Earlier that day Class L1 2-6-4T No. 67754 shunts its empty stock out of the main arrival platform at Withernsea. *(John Oxley)*

A5 4-6-2T No. 69834 arriving at Withernsea with a train made up of two ex GNR London suburban quad-art sets, Sunday 31 July 1955. *(John Oxley)*

Skirlaugh looking towards Hull. The station was a mile and a half from the village of Skirlaugh which is the administrative centre of Holderness District Council. It could have attracted park and ride traffic given adequate parking facilities. In fact it does now have a car park but only to serve a picnic area.
(John Bateman Collection)

A good crowd waiting at Hornsea Town on 2 August 1964, just 11 weeks before the end. If more of these folk had spoken out then closure might have been averted but this was still an age when you didn't question authority. The same people probably accepted demolition of their homes and transfer to 'system built' tower blocks. Anything in the name of 'progress'. *(F. W. Smith)*

York to Beverley – a post mortem

In 1960, BR announced that the York to Beverley route was to become the subject of a Centralised Traffic Control Scheme. As described in *Railways in East Yorkshire (Volume One),* this was in essence a scheme to reduce costs by singling the track, modernising the level crossings and replacing most of the signal boxes with an extra panel in York Power Box.

Although work on the project was begun it was quickly aborted in 1962 and instead the line found itself included in the list of routes recommended for closure in the Beeching Report.

The York to Hull service was one of three singled out in the printed report for a special half page explanation of why they were going to be closed. All the others were dismissed in rather more general terms. This provides an opportunity to consider the reasons for the demise of one of the more marginal lines in East Yorkshire.

Few could deny that by the early 1960s, British Railways was in need of a radical shake up. In what was fast becoming an age of mass car ownership, the railways were widely perceived as a Victorian anachronism. Ernest Marples was, by profession, a chartered accountant (as is the author of this book). Unlike most Ministers of Transport, who hold the post briefly as a stepping stone either to higher things or to oblivion, it was in this post that he made his mark from 1959 to 1964. He opened the first motorway in this country and introduced traffic wardens. In 1961 he appointed Dr Beeching to reorganise British Railways.

It is said in defence of Dr Beeching that he never promised to eliminate the BR deficit completely. The Government certainly hoped that he would. In his Report published in 1963, Dr Beeching sought to achieve a mere 28% of the planned financial turnround by a programme of widespread closures involving more than half the network.

This was the aspect of the Report which received all the publicity and which gained almost universal support. How else could it have been implemented during the middle of a general election campaign? Indeed the closure programme was still in full swing through a second election in 1966. The antiquated railways were held in such low regard whilst people were so mesmerised by their new motor cars that the Beeching Report was accepted without question. Nobody could conceive that the growth in car ownership, far from eliminating the need for railways, would within a generation produce the congestion which is now the very reason why railways are in increasing demand in practically all conurbations throughout Europe.

It was stated in the Beeching Report that the York to Hull line served a rural area with 'an element' of commuter traffic at each end. The following is a summary of the case for closure. The figures are exactly as stated but the layout is my own.

Market Weighton, 4 October 1847 – 2/ November 1965. R.I.P.   *(D. J. Mitchell)*

			£
York – Hull revenue			90,400
Less Movement expenses	84,400		
Terminal expenses	23,100		
Track & signalling expenses	43,300	150,800	
Operating Loss			60,400
Less Contributory revenue to other parts of BR			37,700
Loss after contributory revenue			£ 22,700
Savings from closure			
As above			22,700
Add Revenue which would be retained after closure (28.3% x 90,400)			25,600
Add Contributory revenue which would be retained (87% x 37,700)			32,800
			£ 81,100

These figures must be multiplied by about 12 to arrive at their 1995 value because of inflation.

B1 4-6-0 No. 61011 in charge of the 6.30p.m. (Sunday) Bridlington to Wakefield Kirkgate approaching Pocklington in July 1957. *(M. Mitchell)*

The route retained a mixture of both steam and diesel right up to the final day when B16 4-6-0 No. 61306 is seen accelerating away from Stamford Bridge in the direction of York. *(D. J. Mitchell)*

The information was not subject to any kind of public scrutiny. Under the 1962 Act, the Transport Users Consultative Committee was obliged to consider objections from the users and to report to the Minister of Transport on the one subject of hardship. The decision then rested with the Minister who, up to October 1964, was Ernest Marples the political architect of the Beeching Report. The TUC hearings were specifically barred from considering any financial matters.

We now know, if only from the more recent Settle & Carlisle saga, that when put under cross examination, the BR financial case fell some way short of being convincing. It is now admitted, even by supporters of Dr Beeching, that 'some pretty rough and ready decisions were taken based on some pretty rough and ready figures in the interests of what was taken to be the party line'. 'It was not unknown for lines to be put up for closure using the costs of a steam hauled service which had largely been replaced by diesel traction' (*Modern Railways*, October 1989).

In the case of the York to Beverley line, it is likely that some of the costs were exaggerated and it is certain that others were capable of reduction. Only two years earlier, BR had claimed in support of the CTC scheme that annual track and signalling expenses could be reduced by £12,000. It is possible that movement expenses included more steam working than was actually then the case and

in a few years all steam operation would have been eliminated. Terminal expenses very probably included costs at York, Beverley, Cottingham and Hull stations which would have continued regardless of the fate of the York – Hull service. The remaining costs at intermediate stations could and would have been severely reduced with the introduction of ticket issue on trains. It may also be fair to add that some of the movement costs would, on closure, simply transfer onto additional low productivity Hull – Beverley short workings.

The case for closure depended heavily on the optimistic forecast of traffic that would be retained. The figures must have assumed that practically all traffic from Hull to York and beyond would stay with BR but the service via Selby after 1965 was nothing like good enough to achieve that. Maybe it was assumed that Beverley to York passengers would travel via Hull and Selby which is hardly conceivable. The figures must also have anticipated that longer distance passengers from Market Weighton and Pocklington would go by bus to York then continue by train. We know that this just does not happen.

Add all these arguments together and the financial case for closure becomes more marginal. Unfortunately in the years 1963 to 1966, there was no alternative to the closure policy. After the 1964 general election, the Labour Government continued exactly the same policy as its predecessor. There

Plenty of new housing adjacent to Stamford Bridge Station. The bus is probably doing a good job but it will never get into York as quickly as the train could have done. *(Martin Bairstow)*

was no scope for introducing cost saving measures such as the CTC scheme. There was no acceptance of subsidy. Even had the Minister of Transport refused closure in 1965, it would only have been as a short term expedient because it was no part of Government policy to provide the means of retaining this type of service.

The tragedy is that a more enlightened policy did begin to emerge only a short time later. In December 1965, Mrs Barbara Castle was appointed Minister of Transport. She held the post for over two years and is possibly the only Minister other than Ernest Marples to have made much of an impression in the office. In April 1966, she dropped the first hints at stabilising the size of the BR network and introduced the concept of the 'basic railway' whereby costs would be reduced as an alternative to closure. In 1968 legislation was passed accepting the concept of subsidy. It was not until 1974, that the onslaught of closures was brought to an end but from about 1966, the pace began to slow down considerably.

The Harrogate to York line was reprieved by Mrs Castle in 1966, initially as a temporary expedient but it is still operating with more trains and more passengers. Some costs have been eliminated though as explained in *Railways Around Harrogate Volume Two* there remains a long way to go in that direction. The Hull to Scarborough line was not put through the closure machinery until 1968 by which time the survival rate was comparatively high. It too is still functioning and, with support from Humberside County Council, major inroads have been made into operating costs through investment in level crossing automation.

The York – Beverley route closed in 1965 because it fell foul of the politics of that day. Had it gained even a temporary reprieve taking it into the era of the basic railway, then it could have been developed to the point where its costs were within the limits of what has become politically acceptable. Its story might then have followed the pattern of the neighbouring York to Harrogate and Hull to Bridlington lines. There has been significant housing development along the route at Earswick, Warthill, Stamford Bridge, Pocklington and Market Weighton. It is fair to predict that there would have been even more houses built if the railway had still been in operation. This is certainly the trend elsewhere.

Today there might well have been more than just the 'element' of commuter traffic identified in the Beeching Report.

For through travellers between York and Hull, there is now a credible service via Selby. This came largely as a consequence of the 1983 diversion of the East Coast Main Line away from Selby. As a replacement for the Market Weighton route it was 18 years late.

What was permanently sacrificed with the abandonment of the Market Weighton line was the potential for getting commuters, shoppers etc from the intermediate towns and villages into the increasingly congested centres of York and Hull. Also there was potential for feeder traffic changing onto long distance trains. It is true that a lot of 'Inter City' customers who park their cars at York Station hail from the Pocklington, Market Weighton direction. But it is equally a fact that many people faced with a 20 mile drive into a city centre with expensive parking if they wish to catch a train will elect to drive the whole way to their destination.

The cost of maintaining structures was not necessarily extinguished upon closure. Stamford Bridge Viaduct, seen here in August 1971, is still standing today. York is to the left and Stamford Bridge Station to the right. *(John Marshall)*

The 1929 Hull and District Interval Service

By David R. Smith

D20 4-4-0 No. 62386 heads a local out of Hull, probably for its home base at Selby. *(Lance Brown)*

On 29 November 1928 Ralph Wedgwood presented a report to the London & North Eastern Railway Traffic Committee meeting in London. Although Wedgwood had been in charge as LNER Chief General Manager for almost six years, his continuing interest in matters North Eastern was clearly in evidence. His signed report demonstrates the importance he attached to the urgent need to stem the decline in local rail traffic in and around Hull.

Wedgwood began by pointing out that there had been a steady decline in suburban traffic in the Hull district for over five years. In the twelve months ending 31 August 1923 revenue from local passenger traffic totalled £111,465, but five years later the figure was only £88,208, a 20% reduction.[1]

At that time "suburban traffic" comprised the branches to Hornsea and Withernsea, the former Hull & Barnsley main line as far as South Howden and the stations at Cottingham, Beverley, Hessle, Ferriby and Brough on the two principal lines out of Hull. There was also a significant commuter traffic to stations further out at Bridlington, Filey and Scarborough and (to a much lesser extent) to Goole and Selby but to those places the developing bus

services could not compete on speed and convenience and there was evidence that the impact of bus competition was much less.[2]

To stem the decline Wedgwood reported that consideration had been given to recovering part of this loss by running regular interval services between Hull and Brough, Beverley, Hornsea, Withernsea and South Howden using steam rail coaches at an estimated additional cost of £17,200 per annum, made up of train mileage (£15,500) and interest on capital and depreciation (£1,700).

Wedgwood hammered home the seriousness of the situation:

"It may be assumed that if no action is taken the traffic will continue to decline under the influence of road competition and the further loss by 31.8.1931 will bring revenue down a further £10,000 p.a. On the other hand it is probably reasonable to anticipate that the institution of the interval service may result in a 10% increase in revenue, giving an additional £9,000 p.a., or a total of £19,000 as at 31.8.1931.

"An intensified service, running at regular intervals with such cheap fares as have already been instituted in and around the town of Hull gives the best hope of successfully meeting road competition and there seems no other way of restoring the position in the Hull District."

"The case is typical of what is occurring in the neighbourhood of many of our large towns and it seems desirable to make the experiment. If, after a reasonable trial, the experiment proves unsuccessful, we can reduce the service and find employment elsewhere for the rail coaches so liberated".

Wedgwood concluded by saying that if the Directors gave general approval full details would be worked out for new services to be introduced in the Summer 1929 timetable.

At this point something should be said about earlier developments. The LNER had already embarked on a policy of introducing steam rail coaches (the Sentinel and Clayton cars) as a means of reducing costs and improving services to combat bus competition which had burgeoned in the 1920s. The genesis for this again came from the former North Eastern Railway which had pioneered the use of 'Autocars' – push-pull units comprising an elderly North Eastern BTP 0-4-4 tank engine and one or two coaches. By the 1920s withdrawal of these units was proceeding apace (the last BTP was withdrawn in November 1929) and replacements had become necessary even without the stimulus of bus competition. The first two Sentinel cars ordered by the LNER had been delivered in May 1927 and one of these, No. 21 (later named *Valiant*) went to Botanic Gardens shed, to be followed by five more from the larger production batch of two-cylinder cars early in 1928.[3] As quickly as these cars entered service additional workings were introduced piecemeal into the timetable (a practice to be repeated when DMUs were introduced to the BR network in the 1950s).

Concurrent with these developments, ownership of bus services in and around Hull was being consolidated. East Yorkshire Motor Services Ltd had been formed in 1926 out of amalgamation and/or purchase of several small local bus operators – Lee & Beaulah, Binnington and Fussey being notable examples. Binnington had competed with the Hull & Barnsley Railway between Hull and Willerby with a horsedrawn waggonette from before 1900 and had introduced motor buses on the route in 1914. Lee & Beaulah operated the main road west of Hull serving Hessle, Ferriby, Brough and places beyond whilst Fussey (who ended his days as a garage proprietor whom I remember serving petrol in Thwaite Street, Cottingham) had started a motorbus service between Hull and Cottingham in 1921. There were also the services between Hull and Sutton which changed hands in rapid succession – from independent operator to EYMS and then to Hull Corporation in 1931.

All these developments and others taking place throughout LNER territory were cause for much concern to the LNER Board.

Not surprisingly the LNER Traffic Committee approved Wedgwood's proposals as an experiment and the full Board confirmed the decision at its next meeting.

Meanwhile a separate development, subsequently incorporated into the main scheme, had been moving towards completion. A month previously, on 11 October 1928, Thomas Hornsby the LNER Divisional General Manager (North Eastern) had reported to his local Board[4] that Anlaby Parish Council had requested the provision of a halt on the H&B main line about 1/3 mile north east of the centre of Anlaby village. Plans were submitted for two 25ft long platforms, situated to the east of Wolfreton Lane underbridge and 73 chains east of Willerby and Kirk Ella station. The proposed halt was to be provided with steps and ramps and the Sentinel rail cars working services on this line would stop there. No staff would be provided and tickets, which would be sold in book form locally, would be collected at Hull in both directions. Hornsby quoted the population of Anlaby and Springhead as about 800, of whom 300 lived within two minutes' walking distance of the halt. The bus fare to Hull was 3 1/2d-4 1/2d. An experimental rail fare of 3d would be introduced which was estimated to attract a minimum of 1,500 passengers per annum to Hull and back producing a minimum annual revenue of £38. The Engineer estimated the cost of construction at £275 with an additional charge of £10 a year for maintenance, leaving £28 net annual revenue, representing a 10% return on the outlay. The NE Area Board approved the proposal, which the main LNER Finance and Works Committee endorsed a fortnight later.

Although Wedgwood had proposed that the Hull interval service be introduced with the 1929 Summer timetable it actually began earlier, on Monday 8 April 1929 the same day that Springhead Halt opened. All local services out of Hull benefited considerably from the increased service.

No of trains in each direction [a]

	Spring 1928		Spring 1929		Winter 1935/36	
	W'kdays	Suns	W'kdays	Suns	W'kdays	Suns
Hull – Beverley	33/37	6	50/52	12	43/45	7
Hull – Brough	29	4	43/45	8	37/41	8/7
Hull – South Howden	12	1	15	1	11 b	Nil
Hull – Withernsea	12	3	18	9	13 c	3
Hull – Hornsea	13	3	18	9	14 d	3

a = a handful of trains which ran on certain days only have been excluded in the interests of clarity.

b = 14 on Saturdays

c = 17 on Saturdays

d = 18 on Saturdays

It will be seen that the number increased by approximately 50% in Spring 1929 compared with the previous year.[5]

Features of the Interval Service

Services to Hornsea and Withernsea were basically hourly, at 40 minutes past to Withernsea, 50 minutes past to Hornsea. With peak hour extras

'Sentinel' railcar No. 2136 *'Hope'* in pre 1945 green and cream livery at Selby on the Goole service. The vehicle was painted brown by the time it was withdrawn in January 1948.   *(John Bateman Collection)*

With a horse box as leading vehicle and therefore unable to work push-pull, 67282 arrives at Springhead Halt with the 12.20p.m. Hull to North Cave on 18 March 1955.   *(John Oxley)*

this gave 18 trains each way on both lines. About half the service was worked by Sentinel cars. On Sundays there were nine trains on each line, again half of them Sentinel workings, although in Summer 1929 and subsequent summers all the Sunday workings were full steam trains.

The Hull – Brough service was basically every 30 minutes, at 15 and 45 minutes past the hour in both directions; seventeen trains (40% of the service) were railcar workings. On Sundays the eight trains provided were reasonably well spaced throughout the day.

The off peak service to Beverley was basically at 15 and 45 minutes past the hour from both Hull and Beverley, boosted by trains to and from Scarborough, Bridlington and York; these together with extra rush hour trains gave Cottingham and Beverley a 15-minute service at certain times of the day.

By judiciously retiming certain long established trains to Leeds, Doncaster, York, Bridlington and Scarborough by a few minutes, the even interval principle was substantially maintained on the Brough – Hull and Beverley – Hull sections; the few

exceptions at the outset regrettably increased in number in succeeding years, weakening the rigid interval principle.

On the Hull & Barnsley line, trains worked by Sentinel cars called at Springhead Halt to set down on journeys from Hull and to pick up in the opposite direction. Departures from Hull were generally at 55 minutes past the hour but with exceptions. At this time there was still a service beyond South Howden to Cudworth which also conformed to the interval pattern.[6] The full timetable for this service is reproduced below:

The interval service continued unchanged until September 1930 with the addition of Summer seasonal trains to Bridlington and Scarborough (as had been the case in earlier years and continued to be so for long afterwards). An innovation introduced in Summer 1929 was a service of four Sunday trains between Hull and North Cave, all worked by the Sentinel cars. This was repeated in the 1930 Summer timetable (with one train less) but never reappeared thereafter. The Sunday service to Hornsea and Withernsea reverted to five trains each way for the 1929-1930 Winter timetable.

HULL AND SOUTH HOWDEN — COMMENCING 8 APRIL 1929

WEEKDAYS / WEEKDAYS—continued. / SUNDAYS

		X. a.m.	X. a.m.	X. a.m.	S.O. a.m.	X. S.X. p.m.	p.m.	X. S.X. p.m.	X. S.O. p.m.	p.m.	S.O. p.m.	X. p.m.	X. S.X. p.m.	X. p.m.	Y. p.m.	X. p.m.	X. WSX. p.m.	Y. WSO. p.m.	X. S.O. p.m.	SUNDAYS a.m.
Hull .... dep.	6 20	6 55	7 5	8 30	10 55	12 10	12 10	1 10	1 55	1 55	2 55	3 55	4 30	5 15	5 55	6 55	8 55	9 55	9 55	10 40	10 45
Springhead Halt .... ,,	....	....	A	A	A	A	A		A	A		A	A	A	E	A	A	A	E	A	
Willerby and Kirk Ella ,,	6 30	7 4	7 18	8 43	11 8	12 20	12 23	1 20	2 8	2 8	3 4	4 5	4 43	5 28	6 8	7 8	9 8	10 8	10 8	10 53	10 55
Little Weighton .... ,,	6 39	7 13	7 28	8 53	11 18	12 30	12 33	1 29		2 18	3 13	4 15	4 53	5 38	6 18	7 18	9 18	10 18	10 18	11 3	11 4
South Cave .... ,,	6 46	7 20	7 35	9 0	11 25	12 37	12 40	1 36		2 25	3 20	4 22	5 0	5 45	6 25	7 25	9 25	10 25	10 25	11 10	11 11
North Cave .... ,,	6 50	7 24	7 39	9 4	11 29	12 41	12 44	1 40		2 29	3 24	4 26	5 4	5 49	6 29	7 29	9 29	10 29	10 29	11 14	11 15
Wallingfen .... ,,	6 56	7 30			11 35	12 47		1 46		2 35	3 30	4 32	5 10			7 35			10 35	11 20	11 21
Sandholme .... ,,	7 0	7 33	,,....		11 39	12 51		1 50		2 39	3 33	4 36	5 14		....	7 39			10 39	11 24	11 25
North Eastrington .... ,,	7 5	7 38			11 44	12 56		1 55		2 44	3 38	4 41	5 19		....	7 44			10 44	11 29	
South Howden .... arr.	7 11	7 46			11 50	1 2		2 1		2 50	3 46	4 47	5 25			7 50			10 50	11 35	11 34

WEEKDAYS / WEEKDAYS—continued. / SUNDAYS

		X. a.m.	F.O. a.m.	F.X. a.m.	X. a.m.	a.m.	X. a.m.	X. S.X. p.m.	S.O. p.m.	X. S.X. p.m.	p.m.	X. S.O. p.m.	S.O. p.m.	X. p.m.	X. S.X. p.m.	X. p.m.	p.m.	Y. p.m.	X. p.m.	X. WSX. p.m.	Y. WSO. p.m.	p.m.
South Howden .... dep.		7 50	7 55		10 55	11 55		1 15		2 15	2 55	4 55	5 33			6 55	8 0			10 55	5 14	
North Eastrington .... ,,		7 57	8 1		11 1	12 1		t 21		2 21	3 1	5 1	5 39			7 3	8 6			11 1		
Sandholme .... ,,		8 3	8 6		11 6	12 6		t 26		2 26	3 6	5 6	5 44			7 8	8 11			11 6	5 23	
Wallingfen .... ,,		8 8	8 10		11 10	12 10		1 30		2 30	3 10	5 10	5 48			7 12	8 15			11 10	5 27	
North Cave .... ,,	7 45	8 16	8 16	9 16	11 16	12 16	12 53	1 36		2 36	3 16	5 16	5 54	6 15	6 35	7 18	8 21	9 35	10 35	11 16	5 33	
South Cave .... ,,	7 50	8 21	8 21	9 21	11 21	12 21	12 58	1 41		2 41	3 21	5 21	5 59	6 20	6 40	7 23	8 26	9 40	10 40	11 21	5 38	
Little Weighton .... ,,		8 30	8 30	9 31	11 30	12 31	1 8	1 50		2 50	3 31	5 31	6 9	6 30	6 50	7 32	8 36	9 50	10 50	11 31	5 47	
Willerby and Kirk Ella ,,	8 6	8 37	8 37	9 37	11 36	12 37	1 14	1 56	2 15	2 56	3 37	5 37	6 15	6 36	6 56	7 38	8 42	9 56	10 56	11.37	5 53	
Springhead Halt .... ,,	B	B	B	B	B	B		B		B		B	B	B	E	B	B	E				
Hull .... arr.	8 17	8 47	8 47	9 48	11 46	12 48	1 25	2 6	2 27	3 6	3 48	5 47	6 26	6 47	7 7	7 48	8 53	10 7	11 7	11 48	6 3	

A.—Call to set down passengers only.
B.—Calls to take up passengers only.
E.—Except on Saturdays calls to set down passengers only.

X.—One class only.

Y.—One class only except on Saturdays.

The aftermath

What was the end result? On 23 October 1930 Thomas Hornsby reported to the LNER Traffic Committee in London. Referring to the meeting in November 1928 which had authorised the experiment introduced on Monday 8 April 1929, he stated: "In the 12 months ending 31 March 1930 passenger journeys, representing the bookings at stations affected by the interval service, amounted to 2,053,319 as compared with 1,771,661 for the previous year, an increase of 281,658 or 16%. The receipts in the twelve months to 31 March 1930 were £58,927 compared with £55,341 in the preceding 12 months, an increase of £3,586 or 6%. These figures do not include any increase resulting from the issue of contract tickets". Hornsby added that the percentage increase in receipts was not as great as that for passengers due to some extent to the simultaneous introduction of generally reduced fares to become competitive with competing omnibus services. Whilst the figures had not come up to expectations, they did show that the decline in traffic, which had been going on for a number of years and would in all probability have continued, had been arrested. He continued: "It was thought that as the service became more generally known, there would be a gradual increase in traffic. Since the end of March 1930 the depression in trade and the resultant unemployment in the North Eastern Area has worsened to such an extent that it has seriously affected the revenue accruing on the branch lines where the interval service is in operation. As from 22 September 1930 the services have been curtailed and the trains that were poorly patronised cut out. It is estimated that a saving of £11,500 p.a. will be effected". The committee recommended to the main LNER Board that the curtailment of the services be approved.

If, as Hornsby asserted, the depression in trade and resultant unemployment had seriously affected revenue on the branch lines out of Hull, it was nothing like as serious as the decline elsewhere in the North Eastern area and Hornsby's remarks may have been influenced thereby. On the day the interval service was curtailed passenger services were withdrawn from local stations between York and Scarborough and the closure of seven NE branch lines to passenger traffic was imminent. As the table shows, the cutbacks were in practice not as severe as Hornsby's report may have inferred. Selected trains were deleted from the timetable and others retimed. Whilst a majority of trains ran in the old interval timings, the principle of an easily remembered regular frequency was impaired. In view of the relatively small number of trains withdrawn, the economy quoted (£11,500) was achieved by a judicious mix: more intensive use of rolling stock, conversion of some workings from full trains to Sentinel cars and cutting back Sunday services more drastically than on weekdays. In the case of the Hornsea and Withernsea lines the

A G5 prepares to restart from South Cave for Hull in March 1955.   (J. C. W. Halliday)

Winter Sunday service (now three trains each) was worked exclusively by railcars, a practice which persisted until 1941.

Meanwhile the principal competitor (EYMS) continued to grow, largely by introducing new routes to areas not served by rail and also by drawing some passengers away from LNER trains. How far this growth was restricted by the economic recession of which Hornsby had made such a point is not clear; the financial results of EYMS have survived but the early company records have not been located:

EYMS preliminary figures reported to the LNER Board [7]

	1930	1929	1930 compared to 1929	
			(+ or −)	%
No. of passengers	7,202,456	6,861,676	+340,780	+ 4.97
Car miles run	4,309,966	4,439,963	−129,997	− 2.93
Gross Receipts (£)	189,576	170,477	+ 19,099	+11.20
Expenditure (£)	170,326	155,625	+ 14,701	+ 9.45
Net receipts (£)	19,250	14,852	+ 4,398	+29.61
Gross receipts per car mile (old pence)	10.56	9.22	+1.34	
Expenditure per car mile (old pence)	9.48ø	8.41	+1.07	
Net receipts per car mile (old pence)	1.08	0.81	+0.27	
Ratio expenses to receipts (%)	89.85	91.29		

ø Increased 1930 expenditure due chiefly to a larger allocation to depreciation.

And what of Springhead Halt? Three months after opening Hornsby submitted a memo to the LNER Board. The Halt authorised at Springhead had been completed on 21 March 1929 at an actual cost of £250, which was £25 below estimate and opened on 8 April 1929. During the 12 weeks ending 29 June 1929 total receipts from the Halt to Hull and vice versa were £48, representing 3,840 single journeys. The Passenger Manager was of the opinion that the majority of traffic was additional to rail. No operating difficulties had been experienced in dealing with the 25 foot long platforms but the Superintendent would like experience of working under winter conditions before judging the short platforms and halt satisfactory.

Verdict

Was the interval service a failure? Was enough done to reduce costs as well as increasing revenue? There can be little doubt that it stemmed the decline in local passenger traffic but at a cost. The cheap fares introduced to compete with the buses were not matched by commensurate cost reductions. There is ample evidence of small scale measures introduced by the LNER to cut costs e.g. combining stationmaster posts, removing redundant sidings, closing the odd signal box and so on, but no root and branch attempt was made to bring down costs in any big way by destaffing stations, introducing conductor guards or by using assets more intensively.[8] The large savings which might have accrued from demanning level crossings, of which

G5 No. 67282 prepares to return from South Howden to Hull.

(John Bateman Collection)

there were twelve on the Withernsea branch alone, required technology which was not yet developed in the 1930s. Nor was public opinion willing to move to the less rigorous type of crossing found on the Continent and the USA. Drastic destaffing would also have gone against the grain of public policy which throughout the 1930s depression was concerned to keep as many people as possible in jobs.

Despite its weaknesses, the Hull interval service was a brave experiment ahead of its time. Regular interval services were not developed to any significant degree on non-electrified lines until the 1950s and adoption was still patchy for some ten to twenty years even after that.

Periodically in railway history the charge has been made that railway companies (and later BR) were unenterprising, didn't do enough to meet road competition, were slow at introducing new methods and were averse to regular interval timetables. The same claims were made in the 1950s and '60s and can still be heard today. The 1929 Hull experiment illustrates that the reality was much less clear cut and as such it deserves wider recognition.

Notes

1. P.R.O. Rail 390/1677
2. Other reports in the Public Record Office, particularly Rail 390/1685 refer to the lesser impact of competition prior to the opening of the Boothferry Road Bridge. In the case of Bridlington, Filey and Scarborough the competing bus services could not match the speed and timings of the rail service.
3. Locos of the LNER Part 10B, Page 40 et seq (R.C.T.S.).
4. P.R.O. Rail 390/1674: Provision of a Halt at Springhead.
5. The increase on the H&B line was 25% but that line benefited from earlier improvements in 1928.
6. Departures from Hull at 6.55a.m. and 2.55p.m.
7. P.R.O. Rail 390/816: preliminary bus company results September 1930.
8. In 1937 the average weekly mileage of locomotives on the LNER was still only 104^3/$_4$, despite economies made in the previous two decades. (Michael R. Bonavia: *A History of the LNER/Part 2*)
9. The purchasing power of money in 1929 was about 50 times the level of the mid 1990s.

Acknowledgements
Acknowledgement is made to the sources quoted above and to the National Railway Museum library whose files of timetables were consulted on points of detail.

Push-Pull fitted G5 0-4-4T No. 67273 pauses at Hessle with a local from Hull to Brough in 1954.
(John Bateman Collection)

Class C12 No. 7392 on the 1.45p.m. Hull to Brough, near Ferriby on 26 April 1947.   *(Lance Brown)*

'Hunt' Class 4-4-0 No. 62765 *'The Goathland'* approaching Cottingham from Beverley direction.

(John Bateman Collection)

Expanding The Network

No this is not one of my regular pleas for the reopening of closed lines! There are a number of opportunities for the expansion of railway facilities within the area covered by this book which would not cost a fraction as much as reinstating an abandoned line but which might prove a great deal more productive.

We saw in the previous chapter how 'Trans-Pennine' services have been transformed from an anachronism to something a little more credible in the motorway age. We can now travel by hourly express between Leeds, Selby, Brough and Hull or between Leeds, York, Malton and Scarborough.

But try getting from York to Hull. The present service is certainly as good as anything which has prevailed since closure of the Market Weighton line in 1965 but some of the through trains take up to 1 hour 20 minutes on a Class 141 or 142. This is not an attractive proposition for a journey between two cities which were only 42 miles apart when there was a direct route. It is particularly inadequate for Hull passengers who are changing at York for the North East and Scotland.

With two Inter City electrics per hour from York to Newcastle and one to Edinburgh and Glasgow, also the 'Trans Pennine' to Middlesbrough, there is surely scope for something of a complementary standard to feed in from Hull. Ideally this must mean an hourly Class 156 or single car 153 completing the journey in under an hour which might preclude stops other than at Selby.

The first of the second generation dmus, the Class 141s, were assembled out of standard bus parts in 1984. The 11.49 York to Hull semi-fast pauses at Selby in November 1994. Perhaps this route could merit something a little better.
(Martin Bairstow)

Some Hull-York locals take a detour via Sherburn-in-Elmet rather than use the East Coast Main Line. A Class 142 pauses at Sherburn where the station reopened in 1985 after being closed for 20 years.
(Martin Bairstow)

A Continental connection

Each afternoon at 5 pm a double deck bus leaves from outside Hull Paragon conveying passengers to King George Dock for the North Sea Ferries departures to Rotterdam (Europoort) and Zeebrugge. On occasions the bus is oversubscribed, the overflow having to take a taxi.

There is a rail connection very close to the ferry terminal, a line maintained for heavy freight traffic which could easily accommodate a DMU. If a train ran through from York, it could save one hour on the present journey faced by travellers from the North.

One problem is that such a service would tie up resources at peak times. The ferries leave at 6pm and arrive back at 8am after their overnight crossings. This situation could change when they are transferred to a deep water berth avoiding the time consuming manoeuvre through the lock into King George Dock.

The 26,000 ton *'Norstar'* is a very tight fit as it negotiates the lock leading out of King George Dock bound for Zeebrugge in June 1995.   *(Martin Bairstow)*

Wayside halts

The withdrawal on 20 September 1930 of local trains between York and Scarborough was the first, but by no means the last, example of a whole string of wayside stations being closed on a line which remained open for through traffic.

Amongst the casualties were Haxby and Strensall, the first two stations out of York. Contemporary logic was that these villages could be better served by buses which ran more frequently than the trains and which were partly owned by the LNER.

Over the subsequent 65 years, the populations of Haxby and Strensall have grown out of all recognition. So has traffic congestion in York. The case for reopening must now be very strong. So much so that one of the doubts raised by BR is that there might be insufficient room on the trains for the likely numbers of passengers. It would not be desirable to stop all the Scarborough expresses at Haxby and Strensall which would need through services to Leeds. A possible solution would therefore be to extend the hourly Manchester Victoria – Halifax – Leeds – York local as far as Strensall or, if time permitted, to Malton.

If the problem is finance, then in an earlier chapter, David R. Smith explained how the LNER achieved a 10% return on its modest 1929 investment in Springhead Halt, near Hull. A similar calculation would have been used to justify the small halt at Strensall No. 2 crossing in 1926. New stations today at Haxby and Strensall, though unstaffed, would be a little more sophisticated than either of those 1920s halts. Yet even if they cost £500,000 each (that is 40 times in real terms the cost of Springhead Halt), they would surely generate a 10% return. £50,000 per annum is only £137 per day.

That apparently, is not sufficient. Over the past 20 years, about 200 small stations have appeared or reappeared on the BR network. In almost all cases, the capital cost has been met in whole or in part by the local authority sometimes with grant aid from wider sources including the European Community.

Another fashionable idea is to persuade developers, whose land values will be enhanced by the facility, to make a contribution towards it. There has been talk of such a package being negotiated at Strensall.

On the other side of York, the village of Copmanthorpe has mushroomed since closure of the station in 1959. Here there is the advantage of an existing hourly local service but the cost of a new station would be high. The old one was an island platform sandwiched between what are now the up and down East Coast Main Lines with trains passing at 125mph, possibly faster in the future. Any new facility would have to be on the Leeds lines which might require realignment.

A less expensive candidate is Thorpe Willoughby between South Milford and Selby. This never had a station but the village has grown. Again there is the advantage of an hourly local service passing through. There would be scope for park and ride traffic with people living on the western outskirts of Selby travelling to Leeds.

Hemingbrough, the first station east of Selby on the Hull line, closed in 1967. It was conveniently situated for the village of Cliffe but took its name from Hemingbrough which is more than a mile to the south east. Presumably, the object was to avoid confusion with Cliffe Common station on the nearby Market Weighton line.

There has been housing development at Cliffe leading to speculation about reopening the station. The problem is the absence of a sufficiently frequent local service especially if the present York to Hull trains are superseded by an hourly express.

There would be no problem finding trains to stop at Molescroft just north of Beverley through which Hull to Bridlington 'pacers' pass every half hour. There has never been a station here in the past but the possibility has been discussed with Humberside County Council.

Rail services will always require a measure of public subsidy so the more people who are able to use them, the more these subsidies can be justified politically. The six additional stations just mentioned would, together with a better service from York to Hull, open up the rail network to more people whilst also tending to bind more local politicians to the railway cause.

I am not advocating that the credibility of 'Trans Pennine' expresses be impaired by having them make too many extra stops but there must be merit in taking forward some of the ideas outlined above.

Unfortunately, the privatisation fiasco, with its separation of the infrastructure from the operators, makes it all the more difficult to achieve progress nor does impending Local Government reorganisation help very much.

Since this piece was written, we learn from the May 1995 issue of *Rail News* that 'experts' have assessed the cost of stations at Haxby and Strensall at £400,000 (each or for the pair is not made clear). Annual income is also assessed at £400,000 giving a much better rate of return than that suggested in my narrative. Railtrack are quoted as saying that they would be happy to build the stations if somebody else will meet the cost.

Haxby Station looking towards Malton in June 1964. Although it had closed to regular passenger traffic in 1930, it remained in situ catering for the occasional excursion until such frivolities were ended in the Beeching period. The local population has mushroomed since then. *(Richard D. Pulleyn Collection)*

The previous station at Copmanthorpe was an island platform between what are now the East Coast Main Lines.
(Geoffrey Lewthwaite)

Thorpe Gates looking towards Selby. The village of Thorpe Willoughby, which might generate commuter traffic, is just a short way behind the camera. *(Martin Bairstow)*

Hemingbrough signal box and station remains. It is ironic that this station closed because it served far greater population than some of those which remain open further along the line towards Hull.
(Martin Bairstow)

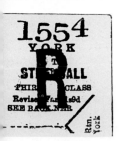

Last time Strensall had a station it was served partly by a primitive petrol-electric 'rail-bus'. In this even earlier view, a Scarborough-bound train has deposited a good complement of passengers including some military traffic. *(Lens of Sutton)*

L·N·E·R

EASTER HOLIDAYS.

SATURDAY, 3rd APRIL

9-25 a.m. RAIL MOTOR BUS

YORK

TO

CASTLE HOWARD

will leave at 9-0 a.m.

AND RUN AS UNDER:

			A.M.
York	- - - dep.	9	0
Haxby	- - - ,,	9	11
Strensall	- - - ,,	9	17
Flaxton	- - - ,,	9	24
Barton Hill	- - - ,,	9	30
Kirkham Abbey	- - ,,	9	38
Castle Howard	- arr.	9	42

The 10-25 a.m. Castle Howard to York will run as usual.

For further information apply to the District Passenger Manager, York (Tel. No. 2264).

YORK, February, 1926.

L·N·E·R

PAGEANT AT SCAMPSTON HALL.

CHEAP TICKETS

TO

KNAPTON

AND

RILLINGTON

WED. THUR. & FRI.,

27th, 28th & 29th JULY

From	Times of Starting	3rd Class Return Fares.	
		To Knapton.	To Rillington.
	p.m.		
BRIDLINGTON	12 14	3/11	4/2
FILEY	12 51	2/3	2/6
SCARBRO' (Central)	1 25	1/10	2/1
WHITBY	12 15	—	3/10
PICKERING	1 18	—	10d.
DRIFFIELD	12 46	3/1	3/1
YORK	12 55	3/5	3/2

Passengers return each day by any train after 4-0 p.m.

CONDITIONS OF ISSUE OF TICKETS.

Children not exceeding 3 years of age, free; above 3 and under 12 years of age, half-fare.

NO LUGGAGE ALLOWED.

The Tickets are available for the day of issue only; they are not transferable, and are available only for travelling to and from the stations named upon them by the advertised trains. If a ticket be transferred or used for any other station than those named upon it, or for any day or train other than those for which it is available, or in a higher class of carriage, it is forfeited, and the person using it is liable to pay the full fare for the journey travelled, in addition to the sum paid for the ticket.

Tickets, bills, and all particulars can be obtained at the Stations; or from Messrs. Thos. Cook & Son, Ltd., 38, Coney Street, York.

For further information apply to the District Passenger Manager, York (Tel. No. 2264).

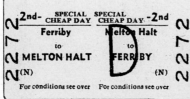

The Swing Bridges

The navigable Rivers Ouse and Hull placed physical obstacles in the path of the railways. Rather than invest in long approach embankments and erect bridges which would be clear for navigation, the NER and Hull & Barnsley preferred to keep their lines at a lower level and so had to provide a total of six swing bridges at river crossings in the East Yorkshire area. Three of these are still in full operation. Two now carry footpaths. Only the one photographed on the back cover has vanished completely.

Goole

The oldest, largest and most troublesome of the six is that which spans the Ouse two miles north east of Goole. 830 feet in length, it comprises five fixed spans together with a movable portion which is 250 feet in length and surmounted by a signal box. Originally there was also a box at each end of the bridge but in 1933 a small signalling panel was installed in the bridge cabin allowing the other two to close. Goole Bridge is now the oldest operational box on BR.

On 21 December 1973, a German coaster struck one of the fixed spans causing it to drop onto the river bed. The bridge was closed until the following August. Due to incomprehensible rules of marine insurance BR was able to recover from the culprit only about 4% of the repair and dislocation costs.

During 1983, BR threatened to close the line between Gilberdyke and Goole, possibly as a means of blackmailing Humberside County Council into making a financial contribution to a programme of repairs to the Goole Bridge.

Just as this work was coming to a conclusion, in the early morning of 23 November 1988 a ship managed to lock itself under one of the spans causing extensive damage. Traffic did not resume until 2 October 1989.

Above: Viewed from the Goole side looking up stream, a dmu crosses the longest of the East Yorkshire swing bridges on 3 July 1965. *(John Marshall)*

Since about 1980, the request to swing the bridge has come by radio from the river pilot who accompanies each ship. The Goole Bridge signalman still has the facility of a North Eastern Railway telescope which used to be his sole means of identifying approaching ships.
(Richard D. Pulleyn)

The *'Resilience'* negotiates the Goole Bridge, probably en route to Howden Dyke, a port which lies about two miles upstream. *(Richard D. Pulleyn)*

The oldest operational signal box on British Railways.
(John Bateman)

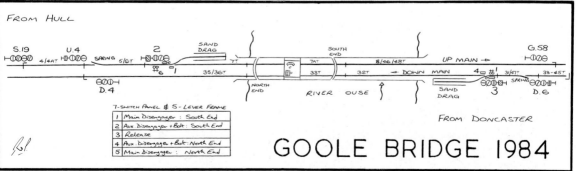

A Class 40 crossing Naburn Bridge in August 1978.
(John Marshall)

The oscillating cylinder hydraulic engine inside the cabin on top of Selby swing bridge. It is powered by a head of water from a tank on the riverside. *(J. C. W. Halliday)*

Naburn

Opened on 2 January 1871, the direct route between Selby and York crossed the Ouse just north of Naburn station by a swing bridge comprising a fixed span and a movable portion 176 feet in length. This was hydraulically driven turning on a ring of rollers at the top of a many cylindered pier, similar to that at Goole.

The pier at Naburn stood on the north bank of the river so that only half of the swinging portion actually bridged the waterway. Naburn lies upsteam of the first lock on the River Ouse and navigation by ships tall enough to require opening of the bridge began to decline long ago.

In 1956 the movable span was welded in the fixed position. This change followed the ending of river traffic to Rowntrees at York in 'trains' of barges hauled by tugs. The signal box on top of the bridge remained in use until 2 April 1967 when the area of York Power Box was extended southwards. The box had originally been only a bridge control box but it became a block post on 3 October 1926 when the neighbouring boxes at Naburn North and South were abolished.

Naburn Bridge now carried the footpath and cycleway which has been established on the track bed of this section of the East Coast Main Line.

Selby

From its opening in 1840, the Hull & Selby crossed the Ouse close to Selby Station by a bascule bridge which could be raised by hand to allow the passage of ships. By the time this structure was replaced by the present swing bridge in 1891, the line was also carrying traffic on the East Coast Main Line.

The swing bridge has a fixed span of 110 feet and a swing span of 130 feet allowing 60 feet of clear water for navigation. Nowadays it is only required to open maybe two or three times per week. It used to be a great deal more.

Operation is from the signal box which stands on top of the swinging section. This was raised by 3ft 6in in 1960 to allow for eventual electrification. That has not happened yet because the East Coast Main Line was diverted away from Selby in 1983 prior to electrification.

The position of Selby Bridge means that the south side gets more sunshine than the north which causes unequal expansion. The solution to this problem was found by allowing piped cold water to drip down the girders on the south side.

The Selby Bridge open to shipping, looking downstream in 1983.   (G. W. Morrison)

The 10a.m. Kings Cross to Aberdeen negotiating the Selby Swing Bridge, in September 1983, a few days prior to the diversion of East Coast Main Line traffic away from Selby. *(G.W. Morrison)*

The H&B Ouse Bridge

Located about seven miles upstream from the Goole Bridge, the Hull & Barnsley crossed the Ouse at a narrower point requiring a bridge just over 400 feet in length. There was a fixed span at either side of the central swinging span which was 248 feet weighing 649 tons.

Designed by William Shelford, engineer to the H&B, the lattice girder spans were lighter than the solid plate girders used by the NER but less rigid requiring a system of knuckle gears and resting blocks to ensure a correct alignment when the bridge was being swung back to its normal position.

The bridge was steam powered, operation requiring a signalman, engineman and boilerman.

These lived in railway cottages on the west bank so they could easily reach work when the bridge was already in operation. But when the bridge had been left open to shipping, for example during the night at weekends, they had to row themselves out to the middle of the river and return likewise if their shift finished with an interval between rail traffic.

After closure in April 1959, the bridge was maintained in working order until 1968 lest it be needed again in connection with Drax power station. In the event, a section of the H&B was reopened to serve Drax but from the other direction. The bridge remained permanently open to river traffic until demolition in September 1976.

The Ouse Bridge looking downstream in 1973, fourteen years after closure to rail traffic.   *(John Marshall)*

The box perched on top of the Ouse Bridge from which the signalman 'must at all times keep a sharp look out for river traffic and work it through with as little delay as possible.'   *(J. C. W. Halliday)*

The Hull River Bridge

With a swinging span of 131 feet, this bridge is also a lattice girder construction. Control is from a signal box on the east bank of the river rather than upon the bridge itself. This ceased to be a block post about 1930 but is still manned for four hours, two on either side of each high tide, except on Sundays when the river is closed to navigation. The track over was singled in 1988. It still carries at least one daily freight train in each direction.

River traffic is now so sparse that it is very common for the bridge man to sit out his four hour shift without having to swing it.

Wilmington

Less than half a mile downstream from the Hull River Bridge is a structure altogether more elaborate in appearance which has recently undergone complete overhaul and renovation. Yet the heaviest traffic which now goes across is a pram or a bicycle.

Originally known as Sculcoates, the present Wilmington Bridge was commissioned on 10 May 1907. It was built alongside the single track swing bridge which had carried the Victoria Dock branch over the River Hull since its opening in 1853. The bridge had been a bottleneck ever since 1864 when the line was doubled to accommodate the Hornsea and Withernsea passenger trains but with interlaced track over the swing bridge which was demolished as soon as the new one had been commissioned.

The new electrically powered bridge was controlled from the overhead box which was never a block post. The block section was between the adjacent boxes at Wilcomlee and Wilmington who, not unnaturally, were prevented from clearing their signals when the bridge was open for river traffic.

Following withdrawal of the Hornsea and Withernsea passenger trains in 1964, the bridge carried a declining volume of freight until 26 October 1968 when the remaining traffic was diverted onto the H&B route.

There had always been a pedestrian right of way on the north side of the bridge which therefore had to remain operational after closure of the railway. In the early 1990s the footpath was transferred inside the bridge as part of the restoration work carried out by Hull Corporation which is now responsible for manning the bridge at high tide.

Two views of the Hull River Bridge taken from the east side.
(Martin Bairstow)

Two views of the Wilmington Bridge, now the property of Hull Corporation, allowing a pedestrian right of way over the River Hull but still capable of swinging open for shipping at high tide.   *(Martin Bairstow)*

The Scarborough Spa Express

9F 2-10-0 No. 92220 *'Evening Star'* crossing the River Ouse at York with the return 'Scarborough Spa Express' on 29 August 1988.   *(Tom Heavyside)*

The charge is sometimes made that steam specials on BR do absolutely nothing for the family market. For a brief period in 1982-85, 'The Scarborough Spa Express' provided the exception.

Operating on about 18 dates in each of those four summers, this was a 'walk-on' service with no advanced booking and no seat reservation. Normal fares applied including railcard discounts and could be booked from any station on BR. There was however a small 'steam supplement'.

The train began at York, where the locos and carriages were based. It then picked up at Harrogate, Leeds and York (again) for the non-stop run to Scarborough. Here there was a stay of five hours before the return trip which followed the same itinerary in reverse.

The first season saw regular loads of 500 between York and Scarborough with 670 recorded on one occasion. Custom certainly included some 'bucket and spade' traffic. BR reported revenue '25% over budget'.

A prerequisite to the operation had been the provision of a new turntable at Scarborough in the pit from which the old one had been removed with the demise of 'normal' steam. Scarborough Council made a major financial contribution to this facility which was commissioned in May 1981. They also paid a small annual subsidy.

The 1981 operation comprised 26 return trips between York and Scarborough, usually one in the morning and one in the afternoon for which special tickets were required.

For 1982 this gave way to the more ambitious operation involving Harrogate and Leeds. I made two trips in August 1982 using my then annual season ticket holder's railcard (since abolished) so it was anything but an expensive day out. Motive power which I encountered was LMS 'Black Five' No. 5305 and SR No. 777 *'Sir Lamiel'*.

Early in 1986, BR announced that the service was unprofitable and would not be repeated. Scarborough Council protested. BR relented in part and reverted to something nearer the 1981 operation. This was repeated in 1987 and on four days only in 1988 after which 'The Scarborough Spa Express' died.

A MISCELLANY

This page upper: Four-wheel diesel railcar No. 294 at Scarborough Shed on 16 July 1934. This unique vehicle helped out that summer on scenic circular excursions to Whitby. It then had a spell on local services around Hull but spent most of its five year life on Tyneside.
(Adrian Vaughan Collection)

Middle: Class Y1 Sentinel 0-4-0 No. 68148 shunts at Bridlington on 1 September 1952, the day the author was born.
(John Oxley)

Lower: The restored booking office at Hull Paragon is now only a facade. Go round the other side and you will find that it actually contains a branch of W. H. Smiths. *(John Bateman)*

CENTRE PAGE PHTOGRAPHS

Left Upper: K3 2-6-0 No. 61890 passing the long closed Barton Hill station, between Malton and York, with a return seaside excursion on 21 August 1959.
(Martin Bairstow Collection)

Left Lower: A Hull to York dmu pauses at Pocklington on the last day of service, 27 November 1965. *(D. J. Mitchell)*

Right Upper: K1 2-6-0 No. 62005, now preserved on the North Yorkshire Moors Railway, waits under what remains of the overall roof at Filey with the 'Whitby Moors Railtour' on 6 March 1965. *(D. J. Mitchell)*

Right Lower: 'Hunt' Class D49 4-4-0 No. 62765 *'The Goathland'* leaving York with an express for Leeds about 1957.
(Martin Bairstow Collection)

The Hull Level Crossings

A Hull to Withernsea dmu entering Botanic Gardens.

(John Bateman Collection)

Wherever they are situated, level crossings are an expensive operating nuisance. Normally the burden falls entirely on the Railway but when there is a concentration of them in an urban area, the local highway authority may assume an interest in seeking to get rid of them and might even contribute to the cost. Such was the case in Hull where, during the period 1962 to 1968, the number of crossings within the city boundary was reduced from 16 to just three.

Hull Corporation had been complaining about the situation for at least a hundred years, long before the advent of motorised road transport.

Originally, all trains into and out of Paragon had to cross both Park Street and Argyle Street on the level causing much inconvenience to the road traffic of the day. With financial help from the Corporation, these thoroughfares were put on bridges in 1871 and 1887 respectively. The move at Park Street facilitated the construction of two additional station platforms.

Prior to 1903, the freight only Victoria Dock branch crossed Hedon Road on the level. This involved crossing the tracks of the Drypool &

Marfleet Steam Tramway. When the Corporation sought powers to electrify the tramway, the level of the road was lowered and that of the railway raised so as to pass over it on a bridge.

Six of the other level crossings were however negotiated by electric trams throughout their period of operation.

The first level crossing to be abolished in the motor age was that at Marfleet in 1934, replaced by a bridge as part of a scheme to provide a ring road around the north of Hull.

There then remained 16 level crossings: four on the Leeds line, one towards Beverley, four on the common section of both the Hornsea and Withernsea lines, then two on each branch beyond Wilmington. Finally there were three on the avoiding line between Hessle Road and Cottingham South. Hessle Road itself was the busiest crossing with the gates closed for road traffic typically for more than six hours in every 24.

The key to the long talked about programme of level crossing replacement was the ex Hull & Barnsley route which skirted the city on an embankment with bridges over most of the roads which the North Eastern crossed on the level.

Hessle Road crossing was replaced by a flyover on 15 September 1962. This required removal of the girder bridge carrying the H&B Neptune Street branch over the NE. A connection was built from Selby direction onto the H&B which allowed some heavy goods trains bound for the docks on the east side of the city to avoid no fewer than nine level crossings by taking the H&B rather than the NE route.

One of these nine, Anlaby Road, which had been the second busiest after Hessle Road, was also replaced by a flyover at the end of July 1964. The three crossings on the Hull avoiding line were abolished when that route closed in May 1965 to be replaced by the 'Cricket Ground' curve.

All the changes so far had been financed substantially by Hull Corporation as was the final push to eliminate the six crossings between Botanic Gardens and Southcoates.

This move may, at first sight, have been greatly helped by the withdrawal of passenger trains to Hornsea and Withernsea on 17 October 1964. However, as speculated in an earlier chapter, it would have required only one curve, in addition to the two which were built anyway, for passenger as well as freight traffic to have been diverted onto the H&B route.

In June 1968, all remaining traffic to the docks was diverted onto the H&B with the aid of a spur from Bridges Junction onto a realigned stretch of the Withernsea line. Four months later, a curve was opened from the H&B onto the rump of the Hornsea branch serving Wilmington cement works. These changes were also financed in part by Hull Corporation.

The crossings at Stoneferry Junction (Chamberlain Road) and Tween Dykes Road had disappeared with the closure of the Hornsea line to goods traffic at the beginning of May 1965.

Of the three Hull level crossings which do survive, two are on the Leeds line between Anlaby Road and Hessle Road. St George's Road and Hawthorn Avenue are not main roads. Both are now worked by close circuit television from Hessle Road box.

By far the busiest surviving crossing is Walton Street on the Beverley line. In 1934 it had become the first level crossing to merit the protection of traffic lights. The traditional gates were replaced in 1962 by 'boom gates' running on wheels. In 1980 the signal box became a gate box rather than a block post. It was replaced by a temporary portakabin in 1987. Finally in July 1989, lifting barriers were installed, operated by CCTV from Hessle Road.

WD heads a westbound freight through Stepney on 17 October 1964, the final day of passenger service.
(Geoffrey Lewthwaite)

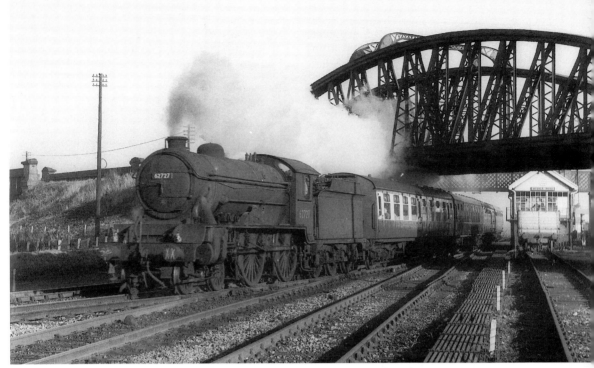

'Hunt' Class D49 4-4-0 No. 62727 *'The Quorn'* passing under the Hull & Barnsley Neptune Street goods branch. Hessle Road level crossing is just beyond the signal box, the footbridge allowing pedestrians to cross when the gates are open to the railway. *(John Bateman Collection)*

Park Road level crossing was located about midway between Botanic Gardens and Stepney. The signal box, largely obscured by the locomotive, served only as a gate box after 1943. A5 4-6-2T No. 69802 is heading for Withernsea. *(John Bateman Collection)*

The Tram Crossings

Of the six level crossings traversed by electric tramways, three had carried horse trams since 1877 without any special protection. The trams simply had to wait if they found the gates closed across the road. This arrangement continued when the tramway across Anlaby Road Crossing was converted to electric traction on 5 July 1899.

However, when the route along Holderness Road was electrified from 10 April 1900, an additional four lever tram frame was installed in Southcoates signal box. The tramway approach was protected in each direction by a lower quadrant semaphore signal and a catch point 20 yards from the gates. When it was necessary to open the crossing for the railway, the signalman would place both semaphores to danger – they were on a single lever – and switch each catch point so as to derail a tram if it over-ran the signal. He would then be able to pull the fourth lever to release the gates. Once they were in position, he could lock them with the release lever on his main railway frame and then proceed to operate the railway signals.

A similar system was adopted later in 1900 at Botanic Gardens, which had never seen horse trams, and at Stepney which had. Extensions to the tramway system involved further signalled crossings at Hessle Road from 1915 and at Newington from 1925.

Tramway closures began in 1931, the 21 mile network gradually disappearing over the next 14 years. The first level crossing over which the tramway was closed was that at Botanic Gardens on 2 October 1937. The last was Anlaby Road on 5 September 1942. Newington closed the same day though it had been used only for empty tram movements since 1934.

A tram recedes along Princes Avenue having negotiated the level crossing at Botanic Gardens. The lower quadrant semaphore for incoming trains is in the off position just above the train which has acquired a canopy since starting life as an open top vehicle.

(Lens of Sutton)

Tram No. 86 requires a policeman to protect it from the row of bicycles as it prepares to swing to the right from Spring Bank into Princes Avenue at Botanic Gardens. This vehicle has been rebuilt out of a 1900 open top original.
(G. N. Southerden, courtesy Roy Brook)

Stoneferry Junction

Situated part way between Wilmington and Sutton on Hull, Stoneferry Box was built in 1913 upon the opening of the short goods branch to the Premier Oil & Coke Mills Siding. At that stage there was no level crossing. Chamberlain Road was not built until after the First World War.

Dennis Coward was a signalman at Stoneferry between 1955 and 1962. His main business was concerned with Hornsea branch passenger traffic but on Mondays, Wednesdays and Fridays there was also the Hornsea pick-up goods.

Each weekday around 1.30pm, the block bell from Wilmington East sounded 1-2 to seek line clear for the Wilmington pilot engine to proceed to Premier Sidings. 1-2 was a local code. The normal 1-4 for a pick-up goods would have had Stoneferry signalling it to Hornsea.

The branch, just over ½ mile in length, was worked on the 'one engine in steam' principle using a brass staff with a wooden handle which was issued to the driver by the Stoneferry signalman. After closure the staff found its way into preservation and is now displayed at Grosmont loco shed on the North York Moors Railway.

Chamberlain Road had developed into a busy thoroughfare with plenty of road traffic heading for the Reckitt's factory, the rehabilitation centre and postal depot.

When there was no obvious break in the flow of traffic, the signalman had to inch the gates across the road in the hope that motorists would take the hint and give way. The object was to have the gates open and the signals pulled off in time for the driver to see the distant signal in the clear position.

This would have been impossible for trains coming from Hull if Stoneferry had waited for the 'train entering section' bell from Wilmington East. So as soon as that box received 'train entering section' from Wilmington Station, it gave 1-2-1 'train approaching' to Stoneferry and that was the moment to start swinging the gates.

In the other direction, it was simple enough if Sutton box was open as the 'train entering section' bell from there gave enough time. However, Sutton normally opened only for the pick-up goods to shunt. It could be opened at other times but only i this was 'in order to prevent delays to traffic'.

If the Stoneferry man requested the porter signalman at Sutton to open the signalbox, he had to be prepared to justify it. As the porter signalman was paid slightly more for signalling than fo portering, the Railway wanted to know why it had been necessary to have the box opened.

Normally, therefore, the block section was from Swine to Stoneferry. Before opening his gates Dennis Coward would wait until he saw the smoke rising as the train restarted from Sutton. In fog o after the diesels took over, he had to allow a time interval after receiving 'train entering section' from Swine.

There was a time around the middle of the day when all intermediate boxes on the Hornsea branch were switched out. It was common practice where box was open for more than 16 hours per day for the gap between early and late turns to be filled by porter signalman who spent the rest of his shift o station duties. Rather than pay signalman's rate t have the porter signalmen work these boxes a block posts, the Railway saved a few coppers b paying lower rates to have them manned only a gate boxes until the late turn signalmen switched them back into the block system.

Until that happened, the section was all the way from Hornsea Bridge to Stoneferry where the signalman had either to look out for the train or else guess the moment to start opening the gates. If h got it wrong then no doubt he would hear either the wrath of impatient motorists or the whistle of the train slowed down at the distant signal – according to which way he had erred.

Stoneferry box closed on 31 October 1964, fortnight after withdrawal of the passenger train. For the next six months, the crew of the pick-up goods had to open the gates for themselves.

From October 1968, traffic bound for the Cemen Works at Wilmington used a new curve off the Hu & Barnsley route onto a short stub of the Hornsea branch which terminated at buffer stops in front o the padlocked gates of Chamberlain Road leve crossing.

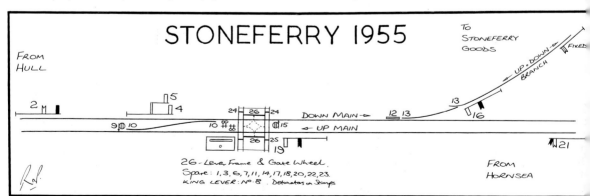

STONEFERRY 1955

The East Yorkshire Trainsheds of G. T. Andrews

By John Bateman

The work of G. T. Andrews, still affording shelter to travellers at Pocklington in 1962. The view is towards Hull.
(J. C. W. Halliday)

George Townsend Andrews was a pupil of P. F. Robinson, known for his country house work, and he won a Society of Arts premium in 1824. Within two years he was established as an architect in York and began to work for George Hudson and the Y & NMR. He then became one of a relatively small number of architects specialising in railway work. His links with Hudson and related railway investments meant that he found himself in straitened circumstances when Hudson was deposed in 1849. Besides railway stations, Andrews designed other buildings such as churches and hotels and he was Sheriff of York in 1846-7. He died in 1855 aged fifty-one, leaving a legacy of distinctive stations to the NER, which had been formed the previous year.

The trainsheds provided by Andrews were a pleasing feature of about a dozen stations in East Yorkshire, ranging from small places like Rillington to large termini such as Hull. The 'skeleton' of the roofs was made from wrought-iron with T-shaped main members and round bar tension rods and ties. The shape of the roof trussing is often referred to as the 'Euston type' since it was first used for the station roofs at Euston provided by Charles Fox in 1837.

Soon after this, Andrews submitted his designs for the first permanent York station, within the city walls, and approval was given by the Y & NM Board in November 1839. This station was the first of his to use this design of truss and set the standard for those that followed. It opened on 4 January 1841. The roof had three spans, expanded to four when a Scarborough bay was added in 1845. The outer ends were vertically boarded to the outline of the trussing and central ventilator. Most of the later roofs were hipped at the ends. They also had distinctive bowstring girders supporting the ends of the roof across the tracks.

Usually a double track station would have a 40ft or 44ft roof span, supported at each side on brick or stone walls. The usual offices were built out from the wall closest to the centre of population and sometimes the stationmaster's house would be tacked on to one end. Most stations had a single span roof but Beverley initially had two spans with intermediate supporting columns between the tracks. The original roof there was replaced in 1908. The termini at Scarborough and Hull also had more than one span.

The cramped terminus at York was the first Andrews station to close to passengers in 1877, but

51

47281 leaving Scarborough with the 13.29 to Sheffield on 4 August 1975. The three Andrews structures were still in use at this time. The original passenger facility is on the left. The two smaller train sheds on the right served as the goods depot until the passenger station was expanded in 1904.
(Tom Heavyside)

The old (pre-1877) York Station still in use for carriage storage in 1964. Originally there had been three adjacent Andrews train sheds but the two on the right had disappeared. The microwave dish on the top of the NE headquarters building is a telecommunications transmitter and receiver replacing lots of lineside wires on the route to Darlington.
(John Marshall)

Malton Station looking toward York in August 1965. Access to the island platform was by means of a retractable bridge.
(John Bateman)

it remained in situ until 1967.

Chronologically, the next 'trainshed' stations to open had been Malton, Rillington and Scarborough, when the York – Scarborough line opened on 7 July 1845. Rillington had been built as the interchange station for Pickering and Whitby but before long this function had been handed to Malton and the long redundant roof was demolished in 1955, twenty five years after the station had closed to passengers.

At Malton the overall roof had originally covered both up and down tracks and platforms. However, the platforms were very narrow and when they were subsequently widened the up platform had to be placed outside the south wall of the station. Large archways were cut through the wall and a new awning built over part of the platform. Thus a single track was left under the roofed section and this served the down platform. A wheeled drawbridge connected the up platform as required. In 1966 the up platform was abandoned and all stopping trains used the former down platform. The overall roof was removed in 1989 and the canopy from the redundant Whitby bay was re-used to provide shelter on the main platform.

Scarborough has been much altered since it was built, although the Andrews roofs are largely intact. The former goods shed had formed part of the passenger accommodation for many years but is now out of use for that purpose. BR installed some very ugly girders on the roof end some years ago but thankfully these have been covered with a cosmetic addition which is more in line with the Andrews theme.

Filey opened on 5 October 1846 with a typical Andrews trainshed, having bowstring ties at the ends. These were later covered over when windscreens were erected on the platforms. The screens tended to restrict movement on the platforms and were later removed. However their use pointed out one of the drawbacks of overall roofs, viz. the 'wind tunnel' effect on breezy days. The footbridge was of standard NER design and did not fit within the walls. Consequently holes had to be knocked in the wall on the west side to accommodate the steps and also to allow passenger access. In BR days the roof lost its 'hips' and was due for removal until funds provided jointly by BR, Filey Town Council, Scarborough Borough Council and English Heritage allowed for

Class A8 4-6-2T No. 9885 leaving Beverley with a Scarborough to Hull train in 1946.   *(Lance Brown)*

complete renovation.

Beverley, Driffield and Bridlington opened the day after Filey, on 6 October 1846. Of these three only Beverley has retained its roof although this is a 1908 replacement for the original one. It received a facelift in 1989. The wooden louvre on the ridge was replaced by a semi-circular cover, which rather altered the appearance from the ends. It has kept its external footbridge.

Driffield had neither a footbridge nor a hipped roof when the latter was removed in 1949. Unusually the roof ends were partially glazed vertical screens, with the usual bowstring girder prominent. Simple platform awnings now suffice, with an interesting arched wall on the up side.

Bridlington started off with two platforms under an overall roof but extensions in 1911 on the east side meant that the original main buildings became isolated on an island platform and both tracks under the old roof became effectively 'down' lines. The roof was removed in 1961 and the whole of this part of the station was sold off and replaced by houses in the 1980s.

Market Weighton opened on 4 October 1847 but lost its overall roof one hundred years later. All traces of the station have now disappeared, but Pocklington, opened on the same day, has survived as a school sports centre.

The interior walls of the trainsheds were often painted white (or cream) with a black base and the paintwork on the Pocklington walls was in a dreadful condition at closure, grimy and peeling. The modern trend, e.g. at Beverley, has been to remove all the paint and clean the bricks.

Hull Paragon opened on 8 May 1848 with a fine stone frontage along its south side and a typical trainshed with three spans. The Andrews roof was demolished in 1904 when the station was enlarged and rebuilt.

	Opened	roof removed	closed	
Beverley	1846	—	—	roof renewed 1908
Bridlington	1846	1961	—	
Driffield	1846	1949	—	
Filey	1846	—	—	roof restored 1994
Hull Paragon	1848	1904	—	station enlarged 1904
Malton	1845	1989	—	
Market Weighton	1847	1947	1965	
Pickering	1847	1952	—	
Pocklington	1847	—	1965	
Rillington	1845	1955	1930	
Scarborough	1845	—	—	
Whitby	1847	1953	—	
York	1841	1967	1877	station replaced 1877 but used as carriage sidings

Pickering and Whitby are not mentioned in the text as they fall within the area covered by *Railways Around Whitby*. During 1994 the North York Moors Railway announced a plan to rebuild the overall roof at Pickering so there may be something to report in a future edition of that title.

Hornsea Station, which features on the front cover, was built in 1864 after Andrews' death but was designed by his former employee Rawlins Gould. The roof is in different style spanning only one track and supported by columns on the outer side. There is however a strong similarity between the Gould portico at Hornsea and the Andrews one at Whitby.

Other surviving relics of the Andrews era include the porticos at Stamford Bridge, Bempton and Nafferton Stations. There are also a number of former Station Houses with their bay windows to let the Station Master see what was going on and numerous single storey level crossing keepers' cottages.

Pocklington Station in July 1973 just prior to conversion into a sports hall. The work which included enclosing the train shed and filling in the space between the platforms, was assisted by grant aid on condition that the facility was made more widely available than just to Pocklington School.
(John Marshall)

A York to Hull dmu under the roof at Pocklington on 28 October 1965. *(John Marshall)*

Beverley looking north, August 1992. *(John Bateman)*

Driffield lost its overall roof in favour of canopies in 1949. A G5 prepares to leave with a push-pull set possibly for Selby or even for Malton about 1950. *(D. Ibbotson Collection)*

A Main Line Bypassed
Selby to York

The southbound 'Flying Scotsman', the 10a.m. Edinburgh Waverley to Kings Cross takes the Selby line at Chaloners Whin Junction on 18 May 1959 behind Class A4 4-6-2 No. 60032 'Gannet'.   *(G.W. Morrison)*

There is one stretch of abandoned railway whose closure produced no opposition from travellers. This was not because the route was ill used. On the contrary it was part of the East Coast Main Line.

Closure in October 1983 of the route between Barlby Junction, Selby and Chaloners Whin, two miles south of York did not even merit the ritual of consideration by the Transport Users Consultative Committee. Abandonment had been provided for in the Act which authorised the 14½ mile replacement route.

Development of the Selby coalfield posed a threat to the Main Line. Even if the then National Coal Board had left a mile wide belt of coal under the Selby to York line, there might still have been problems with subsidence. Instead the Coal Board decided to free the coal reserves by contributing to the cost of a new main line a few miles to the west of the affected area. BR welcomed the opportunity of a purpose built 125mph new line so sealing the fate of the old route north of Selby.

The line from Selby to York included swing bridges over the Ouse at both Selby and Naburn. Historically it did not date back far enough to have been part of the original East Coast Main Line. It would have done so had the Great Northern Railway reached York as authorised by its Act of 1846.

Promoted originally under the title of the London & York Railway, the Great Northern posed a challenge to the monopoly of the existing railways which were dominated by the 'Empire' of George Hudson. The established route from London to York was from Euston to Rugby then over Hudson metals via Derby and Normanton.

Hudson failed to stop the Great Northern but the latter had been forced to spend a fortune getting its Bill through Parliament. It was time to compromise. Instead of continuing its own line through Selby to York, the Great Northern contented itself by ending 'in a ploughed field four miles north of Doncaster' – a description of Askern Junction attributed to the

GN Chairman, Edmund Denison.

From here Great Northern traffic passed over a branch of the Lancashire & Yorkshire Railway to Knottingley then over a short section of the York & North Midland, promoted by Hudson for this very purpose, before reaching the Y & NM main line at Burton Salmon.

By the end of 1852, it was possible to travel from Kings Cross to York in a creditable 4 hours 50 minutes following the present East Coast Main Line to Doncaster then the route just described via Knottingley and Burton Salmon.

In March 1864, the North Eastern Railway obtained powers to build a direct line south from York to Doncaster more or less following the route which the GN had decided not to build in 1850.

Opened on 2 January 1871, the new route was in two parts: from Chaloners Whin Junction, two miles south of York, to Barlby Junction, near Selby and from just south of Selby station to Shaftholme Junction which is close to Askern Junction, north of Doncaster.

Selby was thus placed on the East Coast Main Line which used the same tracks as the Leeds to Hull line through the station and swing bridge.

There were three intermediate stations between York and Selby, none of which were major sources of traffic. The number of passenger tickets issued in 1911 was:

Naburn	7,105
Escrick	8,050
Riccall	10,848

and for comparison:

York	647,264
Selby	125,804

As might be expected, the principal goods traffic was agricultural with the following despatches in 1913:

	tons of potatoes	wagons of livestock
Naburn	4,218	7
Escrick	1,332	30
Riccall	3,543	31

'Bradshaw' for April 1910 shows the York to Selby service as part of the Great Northern main line rather than North Eastern. There are eight stopping trains leaving York at:

6.38 am semi fast to Kings Cross

8.17 all stations to Doncaster

9.27 all stations to Harrogate via Selby and Church Fenton

10.28 all stations to Selby (auto train)

11.45 all stations to Selby

2.48 pm all stations to Doncaster

4.54 all stations to Selby

7.35 all stations to Doncaster

In addition, the 12.15pm from York, the 7.45am 'Through Breakfast and Luncheon Car Express'

from Edinburgh Waverley to Kings Cross made a request stop at Escrick 'to take up first class London passengers'.

On Sundays there was just one stopping train, at 12.25pm from York which was a 'Through Luncheon Car Express' from Newcastle to Kings Cross.

Naburn and Escrick closed to passengers on 6 June 1953. Riccall, which had always been the busiest of the three, survived with a service of only three trains each way until 13 September 1958 when it was swept away, along with many small stations elsewhere on the East Coast Main Line because they were considered too much of an operating nuisance.

Riccall has subsequently grown in population and might now justify an hourly service if there were a regular local service passing through.

The point is academic because in 1979 BR obtained Parliamentary powers for the 14½ mile diversion between Temple Hurst and Colton Junction. This included south to west and east to north curves where the route passes under the Leeds to Hull line at Hambleton. Some York to Hull dmus began to use the new line from 16 May 1983. Transfer of Inter City trains followed on 3 October when the old route was closed between Selby and Chaloners Whin.

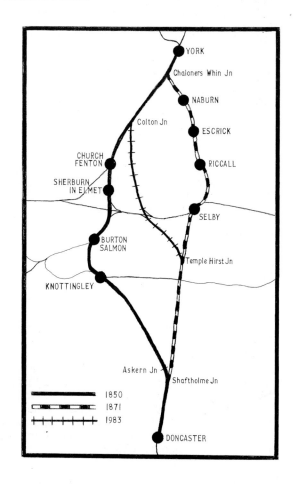

From the demise of steam in 1962 until the advent of Class 43 High Speed Trains in 1978, prestige motive power on the East Coast Main Line was provided by the 22 'Deltics'. 55019 rounds the curve at Chaloners Whin with the 11a.m. Edinburgh to Kings Cross on Sunday 10 October 1976   *(G. W. Morrison)*

An HST crosses the Ouse at Naburn in September 1983   *(G. W. Morrison)*

A3 4-6-2 No. 60073 *'St. Gatien'* passing through the closed station at Naburn with a southbound express on 28 June 1959.
(Martin Bairstow Collection)

40161 heads a southbound freight past Riccall South Box on 18 August 1976. The station was immediately beyond the box and level crossing.
(G. W. Morrison)

The 13.57 York to Kings Cross joins the line from Hull at Barlby Junction near Selby on 22 September 1983. 43092 is the leading loco.
(G. W. Morrison)

Summer Weekends at Carnaby
By A. M. Ross

Under the watchful eye of signalman Arthur Godfrey 'Black Five' No. 45035 passes Carnaby with a return excursion from Bridlington to Marsden on Sunday 30 August 1959.   (A. M. Ross)

I was 14 years old when my family moved from the West Riding industrial town of Dewsbury to the East Riding holiday resort of Bridlington early in 1951. In Dewsbury our house had been close to the ex-L&Y four track main line near Thornhill. Going to and from Dewsbury Wheelwright Grammar School, I passed the ex-LNW main line to and from Leeds, near Dewsbury Wellington Road Station. From our front bedroom window I could see the ex-GN line from Bradford Exchange to Wakefield Westgate, climbing steeply towards Ossett. Immediately behind our back garden was a dead-end goods line, the legacy of an abandoned Midland Railway project to connect Royston directly to Bradford.

The variety of railway infrastructure, traffic and motive power was obvious even to a young observer. By contrast, my first impression of the railway scene around Bridlington was uninteresting and routine. Until, that is, the arrival of Summer and particularly Saturdays and Sundays in July and August.

On Saturday mornings and up until mid-afternoon, holiday trains ran from and to all manner of places, some of them distant small stations which saw just local services during the rest of the year. Not all of these trains started or terminated at Bridlington. Some originated at or went forward to Filey Holiday Camp, a terminus at the end of a short branch opened in 1947 to provide direct access to the Butlin's establishment. Other trains began or finished further north at Filey or Scarborough. Local stopping services on the Hull-Scarborough line during the morning and early afternoon period were few and far between in order to keep paths clear for the holiday trains.

Sundays were different. A procession of excursions arrived throughout the morning until early afternoon. Visiting train crews could then appreciate the seaside delights of Bridlington or Scarborough before preparing for the trek home. The stream of return excursions started around teatime and often did not finish until late evening.

By August 1953, I'd saved enough to buy my first 'serious' camera, which I used initially to record the weekend railway scenes at Bridlington. Seeking a different location and higher speed railway action, I decided to bike out to Carnaby, a small village served by the first station south of Bridlington. The signalbox, at the Driffield end of the down platform, operated a level crossing with a minor road leading to the village. Next to the up platform were railway cottages, the booking office and station house. Beyond the crossing on the up side was a single siding.

Although I was just a teenager with a camera who was not going to buy a ticket, I was made very welcome by the signalman on duty, Arthur Godfrey. The full job title was in fact porter-signalman, because the two shifts worked by Arthur and his colleague Norman Cooper involved running the station as well as the signalbox. In 1950 Carnaby had been put under the supervision of the stationmaster at Burton Agnes, the next station towards Driffield, and Arthur and his family had been able to take up residence in the former stationmaster's house. During the week, the box was 'switched in' for absolute block purposes only for limited periods; at other times it functioned simply as a gate box, giving the signalmen more time to attend to station duties. However, on summer Saturdays, Sundays and bank holidays, the volume of traffic required the box to be 'switched in' operating as a block post most of the time.

Arthur had started his railway career at 17 as a lad porter at Ledston, on the Garforth-Castleford branch in 1933, qualifying as a signalman at Kippax four years later. Spells in the Castleford area boxes at Fryston North, Fryston South and Whitwood Junction had followed before a move to Upton, on the H&B, in 1939. An advertised vacancy had brought Arthur to Carnaby late in 1943. It was a busy station at this period of the war, with a resident stationmaster, two signalmen, a lad porter and a girl porter. Earlier in 1943, a new facing

crossover (points 7 and f.p. locks 6 and 8) had been installed to give direct access off the down main to the up sidings in connection with the construction and opening of the adjacent emergency RAF landing runway. The airfield was vacated by the RAF in 1947 and the facing crossover was removed, certainly by the time I began to visit the station in 1953. The field had later periods of military use before its final closure and the release of the land for light industrial use. The present industrial estate has no rail connection, though the idea has been suggested. It's still an idea and looks likely to remain so.

Carnaby box was 2 miles 95 yards from Bridlington South and 3 miles 198 yards from Burton Agnes. The down starter (signal 17) was a long way in advance of the box. It had been moved there so that a train standing at it was well beyond the 1/4 mile 'clearing point' from the down home (signal 18). This permitted the acceptance of another train from Burton Agnes, though I must confess that I never saw this happen during my visits. Because of the relatively long distances between boxes, a train was not offered to the box in advance until 'train entering section' had been received from the box in the rear. Assuming 'line clear' was obtained, one or two minutes were allowed before the gates were swung across the road and the signals pulled off. The up and down starters (signals 5 and 17) were not interlocked with the block instruments.

On Saturdays, one of the first trains I liked to see was the 9.20a.m. from Filey Camp to King's Norton, which is south of Birmingham. The motive power was often a York V2 2-6-2, which made a marvellous sight and sound as it built up speed through Carnaby. The engine worked as far as Rotherham Masborough via Gascoigne Wood and the Swinton & Knottingley. In the early 1950s, the 11.25a.m. Scarborough Londesborough Road to Liverpool Exchange and the 9.05a.m. in the opposite direction were Selby duties between Scarborough and Gascoigne

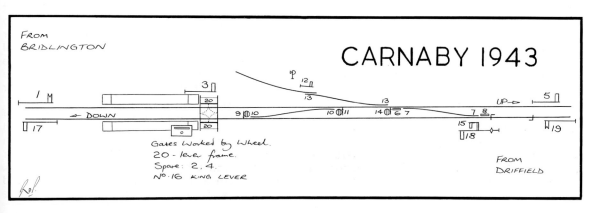

FROM BRIDLINGTON

CARNABY 1943

Gates worked by Wheel.
20 - lever frame.
Spare: 2, 4.
No. 16 KING LEVER

FROM DRIFFIELD

Arthur Godfrey pulling off the down distant (Lever 19) at Carnaby in 1955. Attached to the post outside is the mirror which enables him to watch out for road traffic whilst swinging the level crossing gates. The striped lever on the extreme left is the king lever which can be pulled to lock all the points in their normal position allowing the box to be switched out of circuit but still operated as a gate box. *(A. M. Ross)*

Traffic at Carnaby, evening of Sunday 31 July 1960

Notes and Abbreviations

Cen – Central
Gasc. Wood – Gascoigne Wood (west of Selby)
L in timings – Stop for change of engine or engine crew
Mid – Midland
Mas – Masboro'
Scarborough L Rd – Scarborough Londesborough Road
Vic – Victoria
W in timings – Stop to take water

Type

Addn – Additional
Ecs – Empty coaching stock
Ordy – Ordinary passenger
Q   – Runs if required
Rlf – Relief
REx – Return Excursion
RPEx – Return Private Excursion
*   – Indicates diesel multiple unit

Route

A – Doncaster Avoiding Line
    (Bentley Jct – Hexthorpe Jct)
B – Beverley
C – Castleford
D – Doncaster
F – Church Fenton
G – Goole
H – Cottingham South – Hessle Rd (Hull)
J – Methley Joint Line
K – Wakefield Kirkgate
L – Leeds City
M – Market Weighton
O – 'Old Road' (Rotherham Mas – Chesterfield
P – Pontefract Baghill
R – Rotherham Masboro'
S – Selby
T – Attercliffe Jct – Darnall Jct (Sheffield
U – Tuxford Jcts (ex-GN – ex-GC)
W – Gascoigne Wood
X – Mexborough No 3 box
Y – York

TRAFFIC AT CARNABY EVENING OF SUNDAY 31 JULY 1960

Rep. No.	Cl.	Type	Time pm	Origin	Bridlington Arr. pm	Bridlington Dep. pm	Route	To
Up Trains:								
343	A	RPEx	-	-	-	5.52	BHGD	Doncaster (arr. 7.40 pm); conveys B.R.S. party
261	A	REx	-	-	-	6. 7	MSL	South Milford, Micklefield, Garforth, Cross Gates, Leeds City (arr. 8 0 pm)
-	A	*Ordy	-	-	-	6.20	MYF	Market Weighton, Pocklington, Earswick, York, Ulleskelf, Church Fenton (arr. 7.50 pm); (Empty dmu then to Leeds Neville Hill)
-	A	Ordy	6. 0	Filey	6.23	6.30	MYFCK	Pocklington, Stamford Bridge, Earswick, York, Castleford, Normanton, Wakefield K, Wakefield W (arr. 9. 3 pm)
288	A	Rlf	-	-	-	6.40	B	Driffield, Beverley, Cottingham, Hull (arr. 7.29 pm)
-	A	Ordy	-	-	-	6.50	B	Driffield, Beverley, Cottingham, Hull (arr. 7.40 pm)
-	B	*Ordy	6.15	Scarborough Cen	6.57	7. 0	B	All stns (not Carnaby) to Hull (arr. 7.58 pm)
269	A	*REx	-	-	-	7.10	MSWF	Sherburn-in-Elmet, Church Fenton, Stutton, Tadcaster, Newton Kyme, Thorp Arch, Wetherby, Collingham Bridge, Bardsey, Thorner, Scholes, Pendas Way (arr. 9.34 pm);(Empty dmu then to Leeds Neville Hill)
328	A	REx	-	-	-	7.20	MSWP	(Gasc. Wood 8W37- 8W42) Moorthorpe & South Kirkby, Bolton-on-Dearne (arr. 8.33 pm); (Ecs then to Mexborough).
212	A	REx	-	-	-	7.28	MSWP	Ferrybridge (for Knottingley), Pontefract Baghill (arr. 9 7 pm)
334	A	REx	-	-	-	7.36	BHGA	Goole (8W51- 8W56), Thorne North, Stainforth & Hatfield, Conisbrough (arr. 9.45 pm)
282	A	REx Q	-	-	-	7.43	B	Hull (arr. 8.31 pm)
-	A	*Ordy	-	-	-	7.50	MSL	Selby, South Milford, Micklefield, Garforth, Cross Gates, Leeds City (arr. 9.30 pm)
213	A	REx	-	-	-	8. 0	MS	Market Weighton, Holme Moor, Foggathorpe, Bubwith, Cliff Common, Selby (arr. 9.31 pm)
-	A	Ordy	-	-	-	8.10	B	Driffield, Beverley, Cottingham, Hull (arr. 8.59 pm)
323	B	REx	-	-	-	8.20	BHGAXT	(Goole 9W36- 9W41) Mexborough, Darnall, Woodhouse, Killamarsh Cen, Renishaw Cen, Staveley Cen, Staveley Works, Chesterfield Cen, Heath (arr. 12.15 am)
286	A	REx	7.40	Scarborough L Rd	8.22	8.27	B	Beverley, Cottingham, Hull (arr. 9.16 pm)
330	A	REx Q	-	-	-	8.35	MSWPX	(Gasc. Wood 9W55-10W 0) Kilnhurst Cen, Rotherham Cen, Sheffield Vic (arr. 11.15 pm)
331	A	REx	-	-	-	8.43	BHGAX	(Goole 10W 0-10W 5) Kilnhurst Cen, Rotherham Cen, Sheffield Vic, Wadsley Bridge (arr. 11.45 pm)
552	A	REx	-	-	-	8.50	MSWCK	(Gasc. Wood 10W 7-10W14) Wakefield K, Wakefield W, Alverthorpe, Ossett, Dewsbury Cen, Batley (arr. 11.28 pm)
M991	A	REx	8.15	Scarborough L Rd	8.55	9. 0	MSWPRO	(Gasc. Wood 10W19-10W24)(Rotherham Mas 11L15-11L25) Clay Cross, Wingfield, Ambergate, Belper, Duffield, Derby Mid, Peartree & Normanton, Repton & Willington, Burton-on-Trent (arrival time not specified)
283	A	REx	-	-	-	9. 8	BHG	Hessle, Brough, Broomfleet, Staddlethorpe, Saltmarshe, Goole (arr. 10.42 pm)
262	A	REx	-	-	-	9.15	MSL	Cross Gates, Leeds City (arr. 11. 2 pm)
-	A	*Ordy	8.40	Scarborough Cen	9.19	9.23	B	Driffield, Beverley, Hull (arr. 10. 6 pm)
263	A	REx Q	-	-	-	9.30	MSL	Cross Gates, Leeds City (arr. 11.15 pm)
M690	A	REx	8.50	Scarborough L Rd	9.34	9.39	MSDU	Nottingham Vic (arr. 1.16 am)
284	A	Rex	9.10	Scarborough Cen	pass	9/47	B	Beverley, Cottingham, Hull (arr. 10.36 pm) (Hull - Whitby and Scarborough outwards via Church Fenton, York and Malton - Return scenic excursion)
92	A	REx	-	-	-	10.30	MSWF	(York 12L13-12L30) Newcastle (arr. 2.14 am). Conveys Saltwell Social Club party
Down Trains:								
-	B	*Ordy	5.48	Hull	6.32	6.36	-	All stns to Scarborough Cen (arr. 7.18 pm)
-	A	*Ordy	6.50	Hull	7.33	-	-	-
-	C	*Ecs	8.20	Hull	9. 0	Empty	-	-

Wood and two ex-NER D20 4-4-0s often double headed. The 10.35a.m. Filey Camp-King's Cross and the 8.20a.m. King's Cross-Filey Camp were not quite in the 'Scarborough Flyer' class, but their long train formations were impressive including the only refreshment car services to pass Carnaby. They were usually powered by Hull Dairycoates K3 2-6-0s, either singly or in tandem, and were routed via the Cottingham South-Hessle Road connection to avoid reversal in Hull. And then sometimes there was the sight of a Barnsley shed ex-GC J11 0-6-0 valiantly striving to keep time with the 10a.m. Manchester London Road - Scarborough Londesborough Road.

In the summer of 1958, many local services and some of the shorter distance holiday trains were turned over to dmu operation and Bridlington shed (53D) lost all of its steam allocation, to be followed in 1959 by Selby (50C). Typical Sunday operation at the beginning of the diesel era is illustrated by the table showing the scheduled and return excursion traffic passing Carnaby on the evening of 31 July 1960, with 28 up trains in just over $4\frac{1}{2}$ hours, an average of a train every 10 minutes. The motive power was more varied than on Saturdays, with the engines from distant 'foreign' depots working right through and 'foreign' engines being borrowed for excursion duties. Sometimes excursions would use normally closed stations en route, examples on this 31 July being Stutton (closed 1905), Holme Moor, Foggathorpe, Bubwith and Cliff Common (all closed 1953) and Alverthorpe (closed 1954).

The last passenger services called at Carnaby (and at neighbouring Burton Agnes and Lowthorpe) on 3 January 1970. Arthur Godfrey was able to keep the final ticket issued at Carnaby, a privilege return to Bridlington (fare 6d). Arthur retired in September 1980, but sadly died a few years later following a period of ill health. Remarkably, the signalbox continued in use as a block post and was not closed until 22 July 1990, following the opening of a new crossing, controlled by automatic half-barriers, on a new road from the A166 Driffield-Bridlington route, bypassing the village. The box was quickly demolished, but an arched window frame which used to shed light onto the signalman's desk and train register book was rescued by Arthur's eldest son (also named Arthur) and incorporated into the outside wall of one of the railway cottages, now owned by the Godfrey family.

Between the passage of the pitching 'Pacers' which provide the present day passenger service on the 'Wolds Coast Line', I can imagine myself standing on the down platform at Carnaby, camera in hand, on a sunny Sunday evening in late August 1959. Through the open window of the signalbox, I hear 'ting ting' ('train entering section') on the Bridlington South block bell. Arthur acknowledges and then taps out 4 beats ('Is line clear for express passenger?') on the Burton Agnes block bell after calling attention. Back comes the 'ting ting ting ting' acceptance.

A minute later, Arthur checks that road traffic is clear of the crossing, keeping an eye on the mirror fixed to a post outside the box for any vehicles coming down the road from the village. He then starts to swing the gates. I can remember the rattle of the pawl on the rotating gate wheel gear, the creaking of the rodding and the final crash as the gates hit the stops in the middle of the road. Back goes lever 20, locking the gates. Footsteps are heard across the box, then thuds as levers 3, 5 and 1 are pulled off and the signal wires squeak in their pulleys.

Far away there is a Stanier hoot as the train approaches the up distant, out of sight around a bend $^{3}/_{4}$ mile away. Smoke and steam appear in the distance. The train nears the station, still accelerating, and I can see that the locomotive is a 'Black 5'. Arthur hits the Burton Agnes bell tapper twice, comes to the box window and leans on the rail. I decide on a 'going away' picture with the end of the box in shot. The engine hammers past into the setting sun and I press the shutter release. Above the din, 'ting ting' from Burton Agnes acknowledges Arthur's 'train entering section'. Ten well filled gangway coaches follow the engine, No. 45035. Children wave from the carriage windows. They and their parents have had a good day – fine weather, no traffic jams, no parking problems and a direct service from and to their local stations.

Arthur checks that carriage door handles are secure and the tail lamp in place then throws back levers 1 and 3. The gates are then unlocked and reopened to road traffic. The next step is to call Bridlington South's attention and give 'train out of section' (2 pause 1). Bridlington South acknowledges and offers another return excursion, which Arthur can accept, No. 45035 and train having now passed well beyond the up home clearing point.

I check the reporting number, 514, affixed to the top of the smokebox door of 45035 and to the train brakevan windows, against Arthur's copy of the weekly Special Traffic Notice. The train's ultimate destination is Marsden, in the Colne Valley beyond Huddersfield. It will run via Market Weighton and Selby, with a stop at Gascoigne Wood for water. Thereafter the route is Milford South, Castleford, Normanton and Wakefield Kirkgate. Stops include Thornhill, the nearest station to our old house in Dewsbury. Afterwards, I find that No. 45035 is allocated to Warrington Dallam shed (8B) and can only conclude that the locomotive has been borrowed by the West Riding depot responsible for providing motive power for this excursion.

I gratefully acknowledge the assistance of the Godfrey family in the preparation of this account of a period of life at Carnaby station.

Class D49/2 4-4-0 No. 62756 *'The Brocklesby'* passing Carnaby with a Scarborough to Hull local in April 1958. This train stopped at most stations except Carnaby. *(A. M. Ross)*

B1 No. 61305 passing Flamborough Station with the 5.10p.m. (Mondays to Fridays) Hull to Scarborough express in 1959. *(A. M. Ross)*

A pair of K3s, 61965 and 61922, in charge of the 8.18a.m. Kings Cross to Filey Holiday Camp under the Andrews roof at Bridlington in the summer of 1957. The Dairycoates engines will have brought the train from Doncaster with a crew change at Hessle Road. *(A. M. Ross)*

'The Scarborough Flyer', the 10.07 Saturdays Only from Scarborough Central to Kings Cross passing Londesborough Road excursion station behind Class B1 No. 61053. *(John Bateman Collection)*

'On Shed' Sunday 30 May 1954
By F. W. Smith

J25 0-6-0s Nos. 65671 and 65723 at Malton Shed on 30 May 1954. *(F. W. Smith)*

The best day to see locos 'on shed' was Sunday when the fewest number were out in service. There was no problem in obtaining permits. You had to say that it was for a party of ten but it didn't matter if only three or four turned up. In any case, nobody said anything to you except 'be careful, don't fall down any holes'.

What follows is a list of all the engines which we encountered on a tour of East Yorkshire sheds on Sunday 30 May 1954.

Malton 50F

This was a two road shed on the south side at the York end of the station. It was demolished following closure in April 1963.

Malton shed was not normally involved with York-Scarborough passenger work but supplied engines for goods and branch line passenger trains. The latter activity was down to one turn per day (two trips to Whitby) following withdrawal of the Gilling and Driffield services.

J25	0-6-0	65648/56/71/85, 65723	
J39	0-6-0	64867, 64928/38/47	
D49	4-4-0	62766	
A8	4-6-2T	69877	
G5	0-4-4T	67293, 67332	Total 13

Pickering 50F

The small one road shed had been extended in 1876 to accommodate two engines instead of one. It lost much of its business with closure of the Forge Valley and York via Gilling lines but remained open until April 1959. The building still stands alongside the road which has been built on the abandoned line south of the station.

| G5 | 0-4-4T | 67308 | Total 1 |

Scarborough 50E

The first shed at Scarborough was a small two road affair situated on what later became the site of Londesborough Road excursion station. It was demolished in 1906/7 but had not been used for locomotive purposes since 1882 when a new roundhouse opened. This roundhouse had only limited accommodation and it was soon found necessary to build a third shed comprising an eight road dead end structure, opened in 1890. The roundhouse was then used for stored locomotives. Owing to subsidence, the straight shed was converted during the 1950s into a four road building, the remaining four tracks being left open to the elements. The shed closed from May 1963 but the

A May 1959 view inside one of Selby's two roundhouses. Visible are three J39s, two Q6s and three Ivatt 2-6-0s.

(J. C. W. Halliday)

turning and watering facilities were retained for another four years for engines working in on excursions.

B1	4-6-0	61060/84
B16	4-6-0	61438/45
D20	4-4-0	62389, 62397 (in store)
D49	4-4-0	62735/39/51/56/59/69/70
J25	0-6-0	65714 (in store)
A8	4-6-2T	69867/79/81/85/86
G5	0-4-4T	67289 (in store)
J72	0-6-0T	69016 Total 21

Bridlington 53D

Built in 1892, the third structure on the site, Bridlington was a three road straight shed. It closed in 1958 but the sidings and 50 foot turntable remained available for locos working in on excursions.

D49	4-4-0	62700/01/07
N8	0-6-2T	69378
Y3	0-4-0T	(Sentinel) 68155 Total 5

Selby 50C

The first roundhouse opened in 1871 with 18 stalls and two access roads built around a 42 foot turntable. A second, slightly larger building appeared in 1898 with a 50 foot turntable, the two sheds adjoining one another.

The allocation in 1954 was 54 engines of no less than 15 different classes.

B16	4-6-0	61422
D20	4-4-0	62374/78/81/84/86/95
J25	0-6-0	65675/83/98
J27	0-6-0	65793, 65857/75/81/88/91
Q6	0-8-0	63378/82/95,
		63406/23/25/29/40/49/50/51
Ivatt 4	2-6-0	43052/97/98. 43123/25
STD 4	2-6-0	76021
G5	0-4-4T	67250/86
J73	0-6-0T	68356/57/62
J77	0-6-0T	68406/38
Q1	0-8-0T	69931/33
Y1	0-4-0T	Sentinel 68150
Y3	0-4-0T	Sentinel 68158 Total 44

Hull Alexandra Dock

This former H&BR shed was a two road timber construction which, having gradually deteriorated to a state of near collapse, was demolished in 1927. However, locomotives for shunting the docks continued to be stabled on the site. The usual classes in the later LNER period were J72, J73 and J77 0-6-0Ts. In BR days from October 1953, diesel electric 0-6-0 locomotives began to stable there and eventually replaced all the 0-6-0Ts. Alexandra Dock lost its allocation to Dairycoates in October 1963 but the dock remained as a signing on point and during the week engines were still kept there in the open. The dock itself closed during 1982.

J72	0-6-0T	68673/76/86. 68747/52, 69001/10/11
J73	0-6-0T	68360/61
Diesel/Electric	0-6-0	LMS Design 12115
Diesel/Electric	0-6-0	BR Design 13073/79/80 Total 14

Hull Springhead 53C

The main H&B depot in Hull was an eight road straight shed. Allocation in December 1923 was 122 locomotives which already included 26 ex North Eastern types. The H&B had possessed 181 locomotives at amalgamation the previous year but many of them were life expired necessitating replacement out of NER stock.

By 1950, the allocation at Springhead was down to 28 engines. It closed to steam in December 1958 but continued to maintain diesel locos and multiple units until July 1961.

B1	4-6-0	61215
WD	2-8-0	90011/61/82/94, 90113, 90217/33,
		90352/82, 90429/67/70/78/97,
		90511/71/86, 90623/63/77/88
A7	4-6-2T	69774/76/80/83/84/85/87
J72	0-6-0T	68746, 69003
Diesel-Electric	0-6-0	LMS Type 12113/14/19/21
Diesel-Electric	0-6-0	BR 13070/72/75/77/81 Total 40

Hull Botanic Gardens 53B

The decision to extend Hull Paragon Station, taken in 1897, required the land on which were situated the two original engine sheds. A replacement was authorised at Botanic Gardens so named after a nearby pleasure park, and this was completed in 1901. The allocation was mainly of passenger engines working to the coast at Scarborough, Hornsea and Withernsea, and inland to Doncaster, York and Leeds. The depot comprised two adjacent roundhouses each with a 50 foot turntable and 24 stalls. During 1956/57 it was rebuilt as a straight shed and from 13 June 1959 it catered for diesel multiple units and shunters. It continued in this guise until January 1987.

B1	4-6-0	61010, 61305	
D49	4-4-0	62717/22/41/57/67	
Ivatt 4	2-6-0	43015, 43130	
A5	4-6-2T	69811/36	
C12	4-4-2T	67352/53/71/91/92/94/95	
G5	0-4-4T	67256/80/82, 67337/40	
J72	0-6-0T	68741	
J73	0-6-0T	68363	
H	2-6-4T	67755/63/64/66	Total 29

Hull Dairycoates 53A

Comprising six roundhouses and two straight roads, this was the largest shed on the North Eastern Railway. Extensions completed in 1915 resulted in five of the roundhouses being joined so that all five turntables could be viewed from one end of the shed, a magnificent sight.

The depot was some two miles from Paragon Station near Dairycoates Farm. During 1916 a mechanical coaling plant was brought into use. There was a twin track elevated wheel drop building with hydraulic lifts to lower the wheels to ground level from where they could then be run into the fitting shop.

Dairycoates catered mainly for freight, mineral and shunting work, passenger engines being stationed at Botanic Gardens. At the grouping in 1923 there were 150 engines allocated to Dairycoates increasing to 175 by 1932.

By the time of my visit in 1954 the total had dropped to 129 with WD 2-8-0s having replaced the ex North Eastern Q5 and Q6 0-8-0s, and K3 2-6-0s in place of the B16 4-6-0s. Other new classes included a number of LMS type Ivatt Class 4 2-6-0s and about a dozen diesel electric shunters. Dairycoates closed to steam in June 1967. Then on 21 September 1970 the remaining diesel shunters were transferred to Botanic Gardens.

B1	4-6-0	61074/80, 61267	
J39	0-6-0	64709, 64914/71	
Ivatt 4	2-6-0	43038/53/69/77/78/79/99, 43100/21/22/24/31	
WD	2-8-0	90006/08/09/21/22/30/78/89, 90104/60, 90210/72, 90378, 90430/58/79. 90609/27/46/95, 90704	
K3	2-6-0	61813/14/19/44/46/47/69/71/84/93, 61902/03/20/22/23/34/35	
A7	4-6-2T	69770/71/72/73/78/79/81/82/86	
G5	0-4-4T	67254, 67301/21	
J71	0-6-0T	68232/42/52/84/96/98, 68304	
J72	0-6-0T	68670, 68718/51/53	
J77	0-6-0T	68429	
N8	0-6-2T	69381/85/86	
N10	0-6-2T	69093/94/96/98/99, 69102/06/07/08	
Y1	0-4-0T	Sentinel 68148/51	
Diesel-Electric	0-6-0	LMS Type	12116/17/20/22
Diesel-Electric	0-6-0	BR	13071/74/76/78 Total 102

N10 0-6-2T No. 69096 is flanked by two 0-6-0 diesels, 12117 and 13074 at Dairycoates on 30 May 1954

(F. W. Smith)

Bridlington Shed on 7 August 1958. Most of these engines will have worked in on excursions including 61153 and 61868 on the extreme right which seem to have double headed the 'Sheffield Seaside Express'.

(M. Mitchell)

Evening scene at Selby Shed in July 1957 with B16 No. 61433, a Q6 and D49 No. 62755 *'The Bilsdale'*.

(M. Mitchell)

Gates Galore!–
Memories of the Scarborough line between York and Strensall
By Richard D Pulleyn

RDP takes up duty at Strensall No. 2.
(Richard D. Pulleyn Collection)

The line from York to Scarborough leaves the city by a bridge over the River Ouse and strikes out in a north-easterly direction, across the Vale of York, towards the natural gap through the Howardian Hills provided by the Kirkham Gorge – a glacial overflow channel which once drained the Vale of Pickering.

As a consequence of the flat countryside through which the line passes, the York & North Midland Railway was able to provide level crossings wherever road met rail. Labour was plentiful and relatively cheap. In this predominantly rural area, many local farmhands joined the railway and continued to work on the land or run their own smallholdings.

So it was that, in the first seven miles of the route to Scarborough, as far as Strensall, there were at least eight manned crossings and about the same number of unattended crossings. A similar proportion of manned and unattended crossings could be found along the remainder of the line through Malton and Seamer before arriving at the coast.

The first crossing out of York was at Burton Lane; from 1880, for more than a century, this was also the junction of the branch down to Foss Islands goods depot. The level crossing was a major hindrance to road traffic on Field View, especially when shifts were changing at the nearby Rowntree's Cocoa Works on Wigginton Road and cyclists streamed out of the factory gates. The bicycle has long been a favoured means of transport for short journeys around the level area around York.

With the development of the Kingsway housing estate to the west, traffic congestion went from bad to worse, so it was decided in the 1920s to replace the crossing with an overbridge to carry traffic direct on to Crichton Avenue; this was one of the earliest examples of conversion from crossing to bridge along the Scarborough line. The gate stops and wicket gates were removed, and thereafter the lever frame started with lever number "4": an anomaly which taxed my understanding in early days.

Only a short distance down the line was Bootham level crossing; this was situated at the divergence of the line to Hull via Market Weighton and Beverley. Originally, the gates were worked by a gate wheel but, to simplify maintenance, the mechanical apparatus was removed and the gates converted to electric motor operation, controlled from the right hand end lever of the frame, which had been renewed at the back of the signal box.

Road and rail intersected at an acute angle, making this a dangerous crossing to operate; indeed, it was always thought that this factor would preclude any form of modernisation. Nevertheless, in 1989 the controlling signal box was closed and the level crossing was automated with Half-Barriers and flashing lights.

Beyond Bootham, there were several unmanned crossings, mostly providing farmers with access to their fields. These were known officially as "Occupation" crossings – to distinguish them from "Accommodation" crossings which provided access to domestic properties.

In both cases, the gates were operated by the users as and when required; when not in use, the

Burton Lane Box which closed in April 1989 following closure of the Foss Island branch. The photographer is standing on the site of the one time level crossing. *(Richard D. Pulleyn)*

The afternoon Rowntree Halt to Selby dmu is about to join the Scarborough to York line at Burton Lane on 23 June 1988. Burton Lane box is on the extreme right. *(Stuart Baker)*

Bootham, one time junction for Market Weighton, looking towards York. Rowntree's factory in the background. *(Richard D. Pulleyn)*

gates were normally padlocked to prevent unauthorised access on to the line. Invariably, the gates were hinged to open away from the railway: users were required to open the far gate first, then the near gate, then "STOP, LOOK AND LISTEN" to check that there were no trains approaching. A cast iron notice fixed to each gate reminded users that there was a "Penalty of Forty Shillings (£2) for Failure to Close Gate After Use" – a substantial amount before the turn of the century when the average weekly wage was well below this figure.

If the farmer wished to cross the line with a long or heavy load, or a herd of cattle, he was required officially to contact the local Station Master who would arrange for Flagmen to provide temporary protection from approaching trains; in practice, this was rarely done, although I do recall Flagmen being appointed during harvest time, when tractors and trailers were crossing the line frequently throughout the day. They were also in place to ensure the safety of the Royal Train which passed on its way to Malton, hauled by an A4 Pacific, when Katherine Worsley of Hovingham Hall married the Duke of Kent in 1961.

This part of the line and its level crossings featured strongly in my formative years: from the mid-1950s through to the late 1960s, we lived midway between the villages of New Earswick and Haxby.

Just across the fields at the bottom of our garden, there was the "Monkey Stile" crossing: alongside an Occupation crossing, a public footpath crossed the line so the railway had constructed concrete steps up and over the post and wire fence. This ensured that the gate would not be left open and prevented cattle from straying on to the line; however, negotiating the top step, even with the benefit of a stout supporting post, required the agility of a monkey – hence the local name!

The top of this stile provided an exciting vantage point for our "gang" to watch summer excursion traffic accelerating away from York – although we often ended up with grit in our eyes and soot smeared across our faces from the passing steam trains!

Many lazy childhood afternoons were spent out in the fields adjoining the Monkey Stile. As the sun gradually warmed the rails they would expand with loud cracks like shots from a gun; tar could be seen to bubble out of knot holes in the wooden sleepers.

Just once, I recall how we copied generations past by carefully placing a penny on the rail so that the next train would hammer it into a flat copper disk. When we proudly showed the results of our experiment to the passing Trackwalker we were distressed to be told that this was "defacing the Queen's coinage" which was a serious offence: for some time we lived in fear of the village policeman

Haxby Road lever frame,
repeater block instruments,
diagram and fire extinguisher.
(Richard D. Pulleyn)

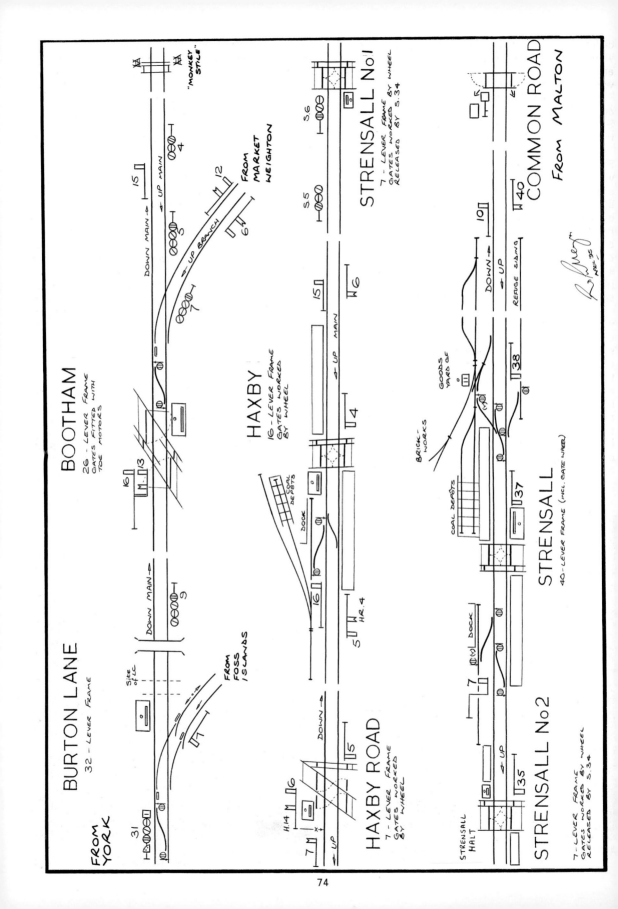

BURTON LANE

32 - LEVER FRAME

FROM YORK

BOOTHAM

26 - LEVER FRAME
GATES FITTED WITH
TOE MOTORS

"MONKEY STILE"

FROM MARKET WEIGHTON

HAXBY

16 - LEVER FRAME
GATES WORKED
BY WHEEL

HAXBY ROAD

7 - LEVER FRAME
GATES WORKED
BY WHEEL

STRENSALL No1

7 - LEVER FRAME
GATES WORKED BY WHEEL
RELEASED BY S.34

COMMON ROAD

FROM MALTON

STRENSALL

40-LEVER FRAME (INCL GATE WHEEL)

STRENSALL No 2

7 - LEVER FRAME
GATES WORKED BY WHEEL
RELEASED BY S.34

STRENSALL HALT

calling to arrest us! I suspect that his real purpose was to frighten us away from the dangerous track, and keep us on the safe side of the fence: certainly, we never transgressed again!

The Down Distant signal for Haxby Road crossing was only a few yards beyond the Monkey Stile crossing; when it was lowered, we knew that a train was on its way out from York.

Haxby Road had been a full Block Post (Signal Box) controlling the passage of trains but in 1925 it was reduced in status to become a Gate Box, simply working the gates and the protecting signals. At that time, the road from York which crossed the railway at an acute angle, was much narrower than it is now, resulting in a wider gap across the rails than across the road; this made it difficult to protect both road and rail, but was solved by an ingenious arrangement which provided two large gates, supplemented by two smaller gates which would swing clear of the road.

All of these gates were worked from a single wheel in the Box: as the wheel was wound, gearing drove a rack or quadrant which, in turn, drove a substantial set of steel rods, connected by a system of cranks under the timber surface of the crossing to the heel of each gate. The gates could be held alternately across the road or the railway by gate-stops, which were raised and lowered by the same mechanism, and could be locked in place by the first lever in the frame; this also interlocked with the levers which operated the signals. Hence the safety of both road and rail users was achieved. As a further safeguard, each white painted gate had red painted "Targets" affixed, and red lamps on the top rail which would shine along the road in darkness when the gates were open for rail traffic to pass.

The gate lamps, as well as the signal lamps, were all illuminated by paraffin burners with corded wicks. A large barrel of fuel was kept alongside the box, and it was a weekly task to refill the vessels in each lamp, at the same time as the wicks were trimmed.

In the mid-1960s, the road was widened over the level crossing; at the same time, the wheel operated mechanical gates were replaced by boom gates fitted with electric toe motors.

The Crossing Keepers were advised of approaching trains by the operation of a single stroke bell which repeated the Block Telegraph signals as they were exchanged between the Signalmen in the adjoining signal boxes: the line was worked on the Absolute Block system, which only allowed one train on a section of line at a time. Even the simple passage of an Express Passenger train could produce a cacophony of sound as every bell signal was duplicated in the Gate Box: "1" beat from Strensall – "Call Attention", "1" beat back – Bootham Acknowledging, "4" beats from Strensall – "Is Line Clear for Express Passenger?", "4" beats repeated – "Line Clear", "2" beats – "Train Entering Section", "2" beats back – "Acknowledged", followed by "Call Attention" and "Train Out of Section" when the train passed Bootham signal box. When trains were passing in both directions at the same time, and trains followed one behind the other, it was quite a skill to "Read the Block".

A Class 150 negotiates Haxby level crossing on 8 August 1987 with an afternoon service for Scarborough.
(John Bateman)

Inside Haxby Box.   *(Richard D. Pulleyn)*

Visual Block Telegraph repeating indicators were also provided to remind the Crossing Keepers about the state of each line at any point in time: one for the "Up" line – towards York, and one for the "Down" – towards Malton. These were small wooden framed instruments with glass fronts placed alongside the Block Bell, on the shelf above the lever frame. Each instrument housed a dial with a telegraph needle pivoted about the centre: when the line was unoccupied, the needle would hang vertically, pointing to "Line Blocked". As soon as one of the Signalmen accepted a train into the Block Section, he would move the needle to the left, indicating "Line Clear" then, when the train entered the section, the needle would be switched to the right indicating "Train on Line", finally returning to vertical when the train had cleared the section.

When the Block indicator showed "Train on Line", the gates were closed to road traffic and the signals cleared for the train to pass.

The crossing was a "Light Duty" post, manned by staff who had been injured on railway service, also known as "Green Card" men because they carried cards to show that they were Registered Disabled Persons. It was a good example of how the railway company looked after its staff, particularly when bad times befell them.

During the late 1950s and early 1960s, two of my friends at Haxby Road were Reg and Bill: both lived in railway cottages at the side of the line, and had smallholdings with a pig or two, a few hens and well tended vegetable patches.

Reg had been a shunter in York Yards until he fell under a wagon which severed his leg above the knee. Despite this horrific experience, Reg remained one of life's ever smiling people: he would lean at

the corner window of the Gate Box and wave cheerily to "his" passing motorists – who were expected to hoot back – and shout greetings to pedestrians and cyclists alike, always happy to pass the time of day. One of his tricks, to entertain the local schoolchildren, was to pretend to knock a large nail right through his knee – of course, the nail simply went through the hinge in his false knee, but the children didn't know that!

Reg was an avid village football supporter and thought nothing of cycling miles to watch his team play – he had a fixed wheel bike with just one pedal; he carried a walking stick on the handlebars to prop himself up just in case he had to come to a stand where there was no handy fence or railing to catch hold of.

Further up the line, but well within sighting distance, were the gates at Haxby station, in the charge of Station Master Jackson and his staff. George and Tom were Porter Signalmen in the signal box; they too were always prepared to spend time with anyone who showed a genuine interest, patiently explaining how they signalled the trains – and reminiscing about their long, mostly happy, railway careers among the country stations north of York.

Although the regular passenger service had ceased back in 1930, there was still plenty to do with the Scarborough and Whitby passenger traffic, the local pick-up goods, parcels and even the occasional excursion from the village. In the summer months, trains would stream by on their way to the coast, balanced by return workings in the early evening. What a pleasure it was, when homework was complete, to cycle out to the station for an hour and to listen to George narrating how life had been as a Junior Porter before the War.

After the goods yard closed in 1965, the signal box was downgraded to Gate Box; Tom stayed on until his retirement, but George moved to the signal box at Strensall station.

Strensall No. 1 gates and box in 1968.
                                    (Richard D. Pulleyn)

The repeater block bell, just to the left of the lamp hanging from the ceiling, in the crossing house at Strensall No. 2. *(Richard D. Pulleyn)*

Signalman George Martin hands the 'last train cautioned' ticket to the driver of a York-bound dmu during temporary single line working at Strensall. *(Richard D. Pulleyn)*

Strensall had four manned crossings, including the gates at the station: Strensall No. 1 and Strensall No. 2 were both "Residential" jobs. This meant that the Crossing Keepers and their wives attended to the passage of trains from cottages which were provided by the railway company; but their wages were low in comparison to other workers, and it was a constant source of complaint that they had to work long hours with very little time off, especially together.

Signalman George Martin surveying Strensall's 40 lever frame. *(Richard D. Pulleyn)*

The cottages were primitive, with outside chemical toilets and paraffin lighting, long after most homes had the benefit of far better facilities. I was shown into one of the cottages one day and was surprised to find that there was a repeater Block Bell on a shelf in the lounge; this enabled the keepers to remain in their home until they heard a train signalled by the adjacent Signalmen.

Strensall No. 1 crossing was on a road into the village from the Army "Camp". One of its keepers was an avid horseracing enthusiast who would take great pleasure advising the troops about the form of the horses and state of the racecourses.

At Strensall No. 2 the remains of Strensall Halt could be found – there were short platforms on each side of the line at which a railmotor had called to serve this end of the village. The Crossing Keeper's cabin was extremely cramped for space, containing a gate wheel and seven levers, besides an antique chair and a stool for visitors.

Originally, both level crossings had controlled their own signals on each line; with the Station signal box as well, this resulted in some complicated slotting arrangements. Eventually, the signals were brought under the sole control of the signal box and the level crossings were released electrically; if the release failed, large keys had to be taken down from the signal box to provide the release mechanically. The pedestrian wicket gates could also be locked by the crossing keeper when trains were approaching.

Up at the large 40 lever Strensall Station signal box, the two Georges were the regular men, both of whom had transferred in when their previous posts – Haxby and Flaxton – had been downgraded to Gate Boxes. What excellent teachers they were –

everything from Block Regulations to station accounts! It was a regular occurrence on winter evenings, when there was a long gap between trains, for all of the Crossing Keepers around to walk or cycle down the lineside to the signal box where lengthy discussions would while away the time. Just now and again we would become so engrossed in a complex debate that it was quite a shock when the Block Bell rang to announce that the next train was on its way; this caused a wholesale rush of staff back to their official posts.

When the Line Manager, Harry, called to pay out the staff wages in the evening, he never complained because he always knew where to find them! He used to say that if you could pass the rule examination at Strensall signal box, you could pass it anywhere.

George from Flaxton was also an adept watch repairer and enjoyed dabbling in amateur electronics, for example by building his own radio sets and a strange looking alarm clock, which incorporated a bright flashing light to ensure that he never failed to rise from his bed in time to attend to the early morning Mail train; this left York at 4.30am!

Also under the control of the Strensall S.M. was Common Road level crossing; again, this was a residential job, the Track Walker and his wife attending to the gates whenever they were summoned by a bell operated by motorists wishing to cross the line – night or day. Surprisingly, the Act of Parliament for construction of the line had stipulated that attendance was to be provided not only 24 hours a day, but also every day of the year! This requirement still applies today.

For the benefit of Relief Crossing Keepers, a small flat roofed concrete hut was provided; there was just enough space for a small stove, an old chair and repeater block instruments.

The gates were locked by a carriage key. There were no semaphore signals, but instead a "Gate Board" – a reminder of one of the earliest forms of signal – which was simply a three foot square board, painted red on both sides, and fixed to a post which could be rotated vertically. When the board was "edge on" to trains it was virtually impossible to see – this was the "All Clear" position; however, when it was facing trains it indicated "Danger". Without the benefit of a Distant signal, it is unlikely that a driver could ever have brought his train to a stand in time.

Postscript

Since 1988, Strensall signal box has controlled all of the level crossings on the line out of York as far as Flaxton: Bootham is an AHB crossing, Haxby Road, Haxby Station, Strensall No. 1 and Strensall No. 2 are all fitted with lifting barriers and operated by closed circuit television.

Given the substantial increase in road traffic, and the need for economies to be made, I have no doubt that the barriers will prove a good investment but the flashing red lights and loud sounding bells are not quite the same as a cheery wave from the top of the gate box steps!

Relief crossing keepers hut and vertical board signal at Common Road.
(Richard D. Pulleyn)

Common Road crossing and gatehouse still in business in July 1995. The board signal has gone but the relief man's hut is still there. Motorists must still request permission to cross whereupon the crossing keeper will open the gates provided no train is approaching. *(Martin Bairstow)*

LOCKINGTON

26 JULY 1986

The result at Lockington when a van was driven into the path of the 9.33 Bridlington to Hull dmu. Eight passengers on the train and one in the road vehicle lost their lives. 59 other people needed hospital treatment.   *(Stuart Baker)*

The flashing lights and audible warning which had been working properly at the time of the accident. The level crossing had been modernised to reduce costs and to allow the line to be open for longer hours. It has since been equipped with barriers remotely controlled from Beverley. Motorists cannot, apparently, be relied upon to stop at a flashing red light unless it is reinforced by a barrier.   *(Stuart Baker)*

Workmen's Halts

K3 2-6-0 No. 61846 passing Melton with a Hull bound freight.

(John Bateman Collection)

Melton

My first trip across the Goole Bridge took place on 1 April 1964 when I boarded a dmu at 1.30pm from Hull travelling all the way to Bradford Exchange via Goole, Wakefield and Batley. The journey took two hours and 22 minutes with stops at all stations apart from Broomfleet, Staddlethorpe and Saltmarshe.

I cannot actually remember the River Ouse crossing. What did become fixed in my 11 year old mind was the train calling and doing business at a station which I had never heard of, one which featured in neither the current nor any previous edition of the public timetable.

On 10 June 1920, the North Eastern Railway's traffic committee learned that Humber Portland Cement had agreed to bear the full cost of building a halt at Melton Lane level crossing. They had further undertaken to pay for maintenance and for any future alteration which might become necessary. They had even guaranteed that a certain number of workmen's tickets would be purchased each week.

In return for these undertakings, the Railway agreed to provide the halt and to stop certain trains there at times convenient for employees starting and finishing work.

Melton Halt had staggered platforms on the up and down slow lines (the outer tracks). When the Hull bound slow line was removed in the 1970s, a new platform was built on the fast line on the Brough side of the crossing.

Even though the halt was unadvertised, it still had to pass through the usual TUCC procedure before it could be closed. Having conceded that point, BR rather strangely began to include it in the national timetable by way of footnote shortly before the end which came on 8 July 1989. Latterly one train had stopped daily in each direction.

Rowntree

Rowntree Halt, near York, opened in 1927 for the benefit of people travelling to and from work and occasionally for parties of visitors to the chocolate factory.

Located just within sight of the main line at Burton Lane, the single platform was reached by a siding alongside the double track Foss Islands branch. This was a freight only line apart from the solitary train which arrived each morning at Rowntree Halt from Selby and the return working in the late afternoon.

Following the loss of Rowntree's freight business, BR initiated the statutory closure

The afternoon dmu for Selby awaiting departure from Rowntree Halt, almost for the last time on 23 June 1988.
(Stuart Baker)

The demise of the Foss Islands branch followed loss of the Rowntree's freight traffic in 1987. Their shunter is seen in the factory sidings on 11 March that year. *(Stuart Baker)*

Another function of the Foss Islands branch was to connect with the Derwent Valley Light Railway whose Class 04 No. 1 (BR No. D2298) is seen shunting at Dunnington, then the terminus, in 1979. The line closed in September 1981.
(D. J. Mitchell)

procedure in respect of the passenger halt as a prelude to complete closure of the Foss Islands branch.

The TUCC reported that no hardship would accrue to the three regular travellers and the train ran for the last time on Friday 8 July 1988. The closure merited four separate mentions in *Modern Railways* including a photograph. In fact it commanded far more column inches than had the Hornsea, Withernsea and Market Weighton closures put together, two decades earlier.

Boothferry Park

Boothferry Park was not a workmen's halt though it was the product of an age when a lot of men still worked until Saturday dinner time then went en masse to watch football, long before many of them had dreamt of private transport.

In 1946, Hull City Football Club had moved to a new ground adjacent to the Neptune Street goods branch of the Hull & Barnsley Railway. On January 1951, a halt was opened with a single 200 yard platform having access direct to the turnstiles.

On match days, as many as eight trains were provided at frequent intervals from Paragon to Boothferry Park and they were there waiting on the Neptune Street branch ready to load up for the return journey as soon as the final whistle blew. Up to 5,000 passengers could be accommodated.

It was also possible to route incoming 'foot exes' direct to Boothferry Park especially after the branch was connected to the main line at Hessle Road in 1962.

The shuttle service from Paragon continued until the end of the 1985/6 season by which time the number of patrons was much reduced, the victim of changing social habits as much as travelling patterns.

BR has never invoked the formal closure procedure. The halt is still there disused but theoretically available for football specials.

DIRECT SERVICE
TO
BOOTHFERRY PARK
FOR
HULL CITY A.F.C.
FIRST TEAM SATURDAY MATCHES

Interval Service:

From HULL PARAGON—from about 60 minutes to 20 minutes before kick-off.

From BOOTHFERRY PARK—Every few minutes after match.

RETURN **9d.** FARE

(Children under 14 years **5d.**)

Suits you " down to the ground "

Ivatt 2-6-0 No. 43069 depositing a crowd of Hull City fans at Boothferry Park on 13 November 1954. *(John Oxley)*

Hull's Own Railway

A WD Class 2-8-0 in charge of a coal train travelling through North Cave towards Hull.   *(J. C. W. Halliday)*

Prior to 1885, all rail and port facilities in Hull were in the hands of the North Eastern Railway and the Hull Dock Company – itself absorbed by the NER in 1893.

Determination to break this monopoly led to the formation of the Hull, Barnsley & West Riding Junction Railway & Dock Company which by an Act of 26 August 1880 was authorised to build a new 46 acre dock linked by rail direct to the heart of the industrial West Riding.

Well almost. The scheme got watered down and plans to reach Huddersfield and Halifax had to be abandoned. The line did not even reach Barnsley but had to rely on running powers over the Midland Railway from Cudworth.

Hull Corporation, a critic of the NER, invested in the Hull & Barnsley securing representation on the Board and a power of veto over any future amalgamation with any other railway. The Corporation was venturing further than most local authorities in its railway involvement. It also made available land on the Humber foreshore for the proposed dock.

What the Hull & Barnsley achieved, when it opened in 1885, was the Alexandra Dock, the embankment around Hull, avoiding the level crossings which so plagued the NER, then an independent route through the Wolds and across the Ouse leading to various junctions with the established railway companies, the L&Y, the Midland, Great Northern etc for onward distribution of traffic.

The route west from Hull involved a difficult climb of six miles mostly at 1 in 100 to Little Weighton. Then followed Drewton Tunnel 1 mile 356 yards in length. This was on a 1 in 150 descent which continued almost unbroken for seven miles to Wallingfen. All this was parallel to the level NER line which followed the shore of the Humber.

Not surprisingly, the Hull & Barnsley had been opposed by the NER but relations improved over the years and in 1899 powers were obtained for what eventually became the King George Dock, opened in 1914, the joint property of the two companies.

Anticipating the 'grouping' which generally took place on 1 January 1923, the Hull & Barnsley was absorbed by the North Eastern on 1 April 1922 becoming part of the LNER just nine months later.

The most obvious change was the closure on 13 July 1924 of the H&B passenger terminus at Hull Cannon Street following construction of the Walton Street curve which allowed access to Paragon Station.

Traffic had never quite come up to expectations and the passenger service was withdrawn west of Howden at the end of 1931. Sentinel railcars and then push-pull fitted G5s continued to provide an outer suburban service until 30 July 1955 giving time for some of our contributors to travel and photograph the route in its dying days.

The line was closed completely as a through route on 4 April 1959. Remaining truncated bits were then 'tidied up' leaving just the high level goods line serving the Alexandra and King George Docks.

WD Class 2-8-0 No. 90478 entering South Howden with a Hull bound freight in March 1955.

(J. C. W. Halliday)

A Hull bound coal train passing South Cave behind yet another WD 2-8-0.

(A. M. Ross)

t Wallingfen, originally Newport, the main buildings were at road level below. A G5 is returning to Hull
/ith a stopping train from South Howden in March 1955. *(J. C. W. Halliday)*

Hull to South Howden push-pull restarts from Sandholme in March 1955. *(J. C. W. Halliday)*

Rights of Way

When the pace of closures was at its height in the mid to late 1960s, it was decreed that local authorities should have the first option on the disposal of redundant track beds.

There are some philosophers who see abandoned railway lines as ripe for conversion into roads but there are many practical problems not least the narrow width. Part of the Hull & Barnsley formation has been incorporated into the M62 near Sandholme and into a bypass around Willerby. The A19 has been diverted onto a stretch of the former East Coast Main Line just north of Barlby Junction, near Selby. In these cases, all traces of the former railway have been obliterated.

The greatest proportion of abandoned railway mileage just lay derelict. The track was lifted fairly quickly and many structures, such as signalboxes, were demolished. Station houses were sold off but there was no market for some of the long stretches of cuttings and embankments running through open country.

Eventually the local authority exercised its right of purchase over a number of sections of route for conversion into footpaths and cycle ways.

It is now possible to walk the 'Bubwith Rail Trail' from the viaduct over the River Derwent, west of Bubwith, to Everingham (8 miles). 'Hudson's Way' extends from Market Weighton to the point where a bypass has encroached the right of way just outside Beverley (10 miles). The 'Hornsea Rail Trail' runs most of the way from the Hull & Barnsley bridge near Stoneferry right to Hornsea Town Station though there is a bit missing where land has been redeveloped at Hornsea Bridge (13 miles).

Part of the Withernsea branch has been converted from the bridge over Holderness Drain half way between Marfleet and Hedon, as far as Keyingham Station (5½ miles). The route can also be walked from Withernsea Station most of the way back towards Patrington.

Finally, the abandoned East Coast Main Line has been converted to a cycle way, of rather superior construction to the others, from a point north of Naburn swing bridge to where the bypass takes over north of Riccall (6 miles).

The principal relics of the railway age which survive along these routes are the station houses which have been sold into private ownership and in many cases extended and converted out of recognition. Some station platforms are still there along with the odd signal box.

I do not think for a moment that the decision to preserve these rights of way has been taken with any belief that they might one day spring back to life as railways. Ironically, the routes with the best potential, the ones which have witnessed new housing development, the lines which should never have been closed such as York to Market Weighton are the ones which have been sold off piecemeal. If there is an exception, it must be the Hornsea branch which is the closest to being complete.

Looking south over the Naburn Bridge early in 1995. Not all the footpaths and cycle ways are maintained to anything like this standard.

(Martin Bairstow)

Corrigenda and Addenda
Railways in East Yorkshire 1990 edition

I am grateful to David R. Smith and to Mick Nicholson for pointing out the following:

p2 The small Burton Agnes box dated from 1875/6 when block working was introduced. The replacement was built in 1903 to accommodate the larger locking frame. Carnaby also dated from 1875/6 but received a replacement second hand locking frame in 1911. It closed on 22 July 1990 and was demolished in October that year.

p9 The down and up slow lines at Gilberdyke were taken out of use on 17 January and 7 February 1988 respectively.

p10 Riverside Quay Station opened on 11 May 1907 and closed on 19 September 1938. It was used again after the end of the Second World War to repatriate German PoWs and to handle leave traffic for the British occupying forces. The landing stage itself had been destroyed by enemy action in May 1941 but new berthing facilities were provided from August 1946 using five Mulberry pontoons of the type used during the Normandy invasion.

Platforms 11 to 14 at Paragon were intended for the pre 1914 emigrant traffic as well as for excursion trains. Emigrant trains took people from Northern and Eastern Europe on a single journey, usually to Liverpool, for onward transport to the New World.

p12 The Selby to Hull line was converted to block working in the mid 1870s. Of the signal boxes then installed, only Crabley Creek and Anlaby Road survived the 1904 widening. Crabley Creek was extended to hold 45 levers in 1901. It was fitted with double glazing in 1989. Anlaby Road closed on 31 July 1964.

Wressle signal box closed on 13 July 1986 and Eastrington on 17 September 1989.

p28 Bridlington Quay to Hunmanby was singled about 1972 but Filey to Seamer not until 1983. Some materials for the latter project were recovered from Hessle Haven box which closed on 27 February 1983.

p29 Driffield Station Gates Box opened in December 1903 and closed on 12 April 1987.

p30 In summer pre 1914 there was a second Sunday train between Hull and Scarborough. By 1938 the Sunday service comprised three trains in winter (two Hull-Scarborough, one Hull-Bridlington) with a more intensive service of up to 12 trains in mid-summer.

p36 Sunday trains ran between Hull, Market Weighton and York in the summers of 1938 and 1939.

p38 The York to Bridlington summer Sunday working was often duplicated so the costs of opening were shared between two trains.

p40 The 1968 curve from the H&B onto the rump of the Hornsea branch was from Burleigh Street North situated to the north west of the H&B bridge over the NER Hornsea line. The curve gave a direct run on to the branch from the direction of the Hull River Bridge.

The 1864 Wilmington station was just on the Hornsea branch, south west (rather than north east) of the H&B bridge.

Stoneferry was at the junction for the Premier Sidings branch, not at the end of it.

p49 Winestead Sidings were disconnected on 29 April 1956.

p51 The train in the photograph is probably the 6.45pm (Sundays) from Hull to Hornsea which stopped at Swine.

p52 Other sources quote 1972 as the year the cement traffic ceased.

p56 Goole Bridge was hit by a ship on Wednesday 23 November 1988.

p58 Sentinel railcars were introduced at Hull in 1927/8. Springhead Halt opened in April 1929 to coincide with the launch of the Hull interval service. Willerby & Kirk Ella was simply Willerby in the H&B days. It was located in the centre of Willerby. Kirk Ella was 3/4 mile away.

p59 North Cave station was 1/4 mile from the centre of the village.

p59 Trains did not just change engines at Sandholme. They were split into manageable loads for the more difficult journey over the Wolds.

p60 In 1929 there were 16 or 17 departures from Hull in the direction of South Howden. The lower photo shows a G5 propelling an afternoon train from Hull to South Howden. The majority of push-pull trains on this route were propelled out of Hull.

p62 The lower photo is of Carlton Towers looking west.

p78 The line between Hull and Wilmington closed on 28 October 1968 and thence to Southcoates on 19 December 1968.

p79 Closure from Hessle Road to Cottingham South Junction was 23 May 1965.

Closed to ordinary passenger traffic in 1930, Castle Howard Station was converted in 1935 so that the waiting room on the York-bound platform could be used in the same way as a camping coach. (D. Thompson)

Links with Goole

The Appendices to *Railways in East Yorkshire (Volume One)* omitted to give dates for the two routes featured in the chapter 'Links with Goole'.

Gilberdyke - Goole		Miles	Stations	Opened	Closed
opened		0	Gilberdyke	1.7.1840	—
2. 8.1869		3³/₄	Saltmarshe	2.8.1869	—
		6³/₄	Goole	29.3.1848	—
Selby - Goole					
1.11.1910	opened to goods				
1. 5.1912	opened to passengers	0	Selby	18.9.1834	—
13.6.1964	closed to passengers	3¹/₂	Barlow	1.5.1912	13.6.1964
	closed to goods	6	Drax Hales	1.5.1912	13.6.1964
13.6.1964	Barlow - Goole	8¹/₄	Airmyn & Rawcliffe	1.5.1912	13.6.1964
c1990	Selby - Barlow	12	Goole	29.3.1848	—

G5 0-4-4T No. 67250 at Goole with the Selby push-pull on 3 August 1957.   *(Lance Brown)*

And finally a word of thanks to my colleagues at Sutcliffe & Riley, Chartered Accountants, Halifax, who not only tolerate my extra curricula activities, but even allow me to fill the office with unsold stock.

If any readers feel that they might benefit from our services: audit, accountancy, taxation or any other kind of financial advice, business or personal, then please give me a ring on 01422 352267 or at home on 0113 256 2711. Distance is no object especially if I can reach clients by train!